The Business of Dog Walking

How To Make A Living Doing What You Love

Veronica Boutelle

Dogwise™ Publishing

Wenatchee, Washington U.S.A.

The Business Of Dog Walking
How To Make A Living Doing What You Love
Veronica Boutelle

Dogwise Publishing
A Division of Direct Book Service, Inc.
403 South Mission Street, Wenatchee, Washington 98801
1-509-663-9115, 1-800-776-2665
www.dogwisepublishing.com / info@dogwisepublishing.com

© 2013 Veronica Boutelle
Graphic design: Lindsay Peternell
Cover design: Dan Phairas

Library of Congress Cataloging-in-Publication Data

Boutelle, Veronica.
  The business of dog walking : how to make a living doing what you love / Veronica Boutelle.
     pages cm
  Includes index.
  ISBN 978-1-61781-128-9
  1. Dog walking--Vocational guidance. 2. Dogs--Services for. 3. Dogs--Behavior. I. Title.
  SF426.55.B68 2013
  636.7'0832--dc23
                                        2013022722

ISBN: 978-1-61781-128-9

Printed in the U.S.A.

Dedication

To Kim Moeller, my Dog Walking Academy partner in crime, first and foremost. The idea of a training and certification program for professional dog walkers was Kim's idea, and I have thoroughly enjoyed the 10 years we've spent developing and teaching it together. Here's to another 10!

To all of our dog*tec Dog Walking Academy instructors for their incredible talents, and their dedication to excellence in training, teaching, and all things dog.

And to all of the amazing dogs, those still with us and those who have passed, who have helped us teach over 600 professional dog walkers across the country. (We miss you Mocha, Jesse James, and Alice.)

TABLE OF CONTENTS

Introduction

Why this book?

People laugh sometimes when I tell them I teach a certification program for dog walkers.

"Really?" they ask incredulously. "How hard can dog walking be?"

The answer is that it's a lot more complicated than people realize. Factor in squirrels, cats, and other dogs. Consider dogs with leash reactivity or a fear of strangers. Or dogs who like to chase things, including bicycles and skateboards. Imagine little kids with outstretched hands and adults with fear on their faces. Then throw in narrow sidewalks or off-leash trails, depending on where you live. Oh, and don't forget that you have to run the business, too. There's an awful lot to learn (and unlearn) about the dogs themselves in order to keep them safe, protect your liability, and ensure you enjoy your job.

So yes, there's more to dog walking than might be immediately obvious. But you probably know this; that's why you're holding this book.

Why me?

When I was Director of Behavior and Training for the San Francisco SPCA, the world-renowned Academy for Dog Trainers was part of my department. One of our staff trainers suggested we start an Academy for Dog Walkers. The shelter declined, but professional dog walking was exploding in the San Francisco Bay Area, and to take a walk on any beach or trail made it plainly clear how complicated dog walking can be, and how much skill and knowledge is involved in doing it well and safely.

So when I started dog*tec in 2003 to help dog professionals succeed in their businesses, we launched the Dog Walking Academy as one of our first programs. As I write now, ten years later, we have over 700 graduates walking dogs throughout the country (and in countries as diverse as New Zealand, Switzerland, and South Korea), and highly qualified instructors in ten locations and counting across the US and Canada. Our curriculum covers learning theory, canine body language, aggression, fight protocols, basic dog training, leash handling, pack management, pack screening, and successful business practices, including client interviewing, client communication, pricing and policies, marketing, and business set up.

This book is based on the Dog Walking Academy course curriculum and contains all the tips and advice we've developed over the years since we began the program in early 2004. My hope is that the information will help you set up a safe, dog- and people-friendly, enjoyable, and profitable dog walking business that not only provides you with steady income, but is a walking (no pun intended, of course) advertisement for professionalism and responsibility in this growing industry.

A thank you to Dog Walking Academy instructors

I'm a quality control freak. When Kim Moeller (who had the original idea for the Dog Walking Academy) and I first created the program and began to teach it in the San Francisco Bay Area, I never could have imagined it spreading across the country, largely because I couldn't have imagined handing it over to anyone else to teach. But over time I've had occasion through my work at dog*tec to come into contact with amazing dog trainers who are also superb teachers. I first knew we'd expand when I met Denise Mazzola. She taught the first DWAs on the East Coast. Then it was Linda McVay and Andrea Stone in Seattle, followed by Lisa and Brad Waggoner in South Carolina. This last year we've added Nan Arthur and Chey Anne Tamashiro in San Diego, Kim Buchanan in Indianapolis, Kimberly Burgan in Austin, and Erin Moore in Vancouver, Canada. We're excited to see where the Dog Walking Academy takes us next.

You can read our instructors' bios and view an up-to-date list of instructors and locations on the dog*tec website: www.dogtec.org.

Chapter 1

Dog Walking For Profit

What is dog walking?

Dog walking is an ongoing service for busy people, rather than vacation relief pet-sitting visits or walks. Walkers provide dogs with much-needed exercise and companionship during the long day while their owners work. And walkers provide their human clients with guilt relief, peace of mind, and a well-behaved dog to come home to at the end of the day, one that's ready to curl up on the couch with them instead of demanding a neighborhood marathon.

The service comes in various formats, and which ones you offer is likely to be largely dictated by your geographical location. For example, dog walking in the California Bay Area usually refers to walking small groups of dogs off leash on beaches or trails, or in parks. Dog walking in New York City is more generally associated with walking groups of dogs on leash down the sidewalk. And in most urban and suburban areas, dog walking means single or small group on-leash walks. What is consistent across all iterations is that dogs romp with their walkers on a regular, ongoing basis.

Is it right for you?

Before you start your business or dive deeper into financial and legal commitments with an existing one, take a few moments to consider whether you are truly heading in a direction that is right for you.

It's easy to glamorize the benefits of being one's own boss—the flexible scheduling, being able to do things the way you see fit, being in control of your own destiny. When a business is running well all this is true. But the downsides are equally important—there's no one to write your monthly paycheck, no set hours and accountability to make sure the unexciting but necessary administrative tasks are completed, and the business's success or failure rests on your shoulders. Many people find working for themselves more of a challenge than anticipated, and it seems that some personalities are better suited to the life of a small business owner than others.

The first self-assessment you need make is how comfortable you are about taking risks. What if you have to dip into your savings or borrow money—as almost all new business owners have to? Does the mere thought of that give you the heebie-jeebies? Starting a dog walking business takes less capital than most enterprises, but you still run the risk of losing money and possibly failing. It takes tenacity and perspective to face such prospects and still work hard and enthusiastically. I've seen many dog walkers quit or go back to part-time work long before their businesses could reasonably have been expected to succeed.

The second self-assessment has to do with your ability to problem solve and your level of self-discipline. You will face challenges and problems throughout your business career. While you don't have to enjoy solving problems, you need to be willing to tackle them head on and not sweep them under the rug. You also need to be self-disciplined, especially about those parts of the business above and beyond dealing with dogs, such as marketing, bookkeeping, and following up with clients. Can you handle a variety of tasks? Do you stick with your plans over time? Could you see yourself doing this in five years? If you've answered yes to most of these, self-employment could be perfect for you.

Reality check: do you really get paid to play with dogs all day?

You do indeed. But you also have to do it in bad weather, and even if your feet hurt. There's more driving than most people realize, and no sick pay when you come down with the flu. And if you like to run off on spontaneous vacations, you're out of luck.

Oh, and don't forget that you have to actually run the business after you come home from your day of playing with the dogs.

If you're already in business for yourself, you've probably experienced some of the frustrations and pitfalls, not the least of which is waking up to realize that your business is running you, rather than the other way around. This common phenomenon can sneak up on you easily, a combination of early systems failing under the weight of increased business, of decisions that made perfect sense at the beginning coming back to haunt you as the business grows, and the press of day-to-day activities stealing away your attention from the big-picture needs of your enterprise. If you're already knee-deep in these stressors, this book can help you dig yourself out and create a fresh start. And if you're just getting started, the aim is to help you start off in control and stay there.

Can I really make a living?

Absolutely. In fact, of all the dog-related services, dog walking is generally the most easily lucrative. There are a number of reasons for this. One, there's no revolving door. For example, dog trainers who see their clients for a short period of time, hopefully solve the clients' problems, and then send them on their way, have to continually market to fill their schedules with new clients. By contrast, because dog walking is an ongoing service, once you have brought in a client (if you do your job well and nurture the relationship), you should benefit from this client for many years.

Two, you don't need many clients to begin with, because you can only walk so many dogs in a day. Three, start up costs are very low. Other than purchasing a vehicle if you need one, you are not likely to need to borrow money to get started as you might for a daycare, training, or boarding facility. And four, the business carries very low overhead. You don't need to pay rent and utilities for a facility, and supplies are minimal (leashes, treats, good walking shoes, and rain gear, basically), so your main expenses will be gas and vehicle maintenance.

What can you make? The actual number will depend on rates in your area and which type of service you provide (off-leash groups, on-leash individual walks, etc.), but generally our clients make between $40-60K annually, with many of the larger businesses that employ several dog walkers making six figures.

Chapter 2

How Dogs Learn

Why start a dog walking book with learning theory? Because, like all animals, dogs have minds of their own. And the better you understand how they think, the more you're able to help them make the right decisions—about when to come running, whether to pull on the leash or walk calmly, which things really need to be barked at. If you don't understand dogs, it's easy to make poor decisions—about how best to train them, or solve a problem, or interpret and respond to a behavior. Your job is to keep the dogs in your care safe while showing them a good time. You should strive to understand everything you can about them and, in particular, how their minds work. Some things about how dogs' minds work may surprise you. Dogs are similar to us in many ways, but understanding the differences is key to being a successful dog walker.

Dogs, like all learning organisms, learn in two ways. Learning by association explains why dogs jump for joy at the sight of a leash and run at the sight of nail clippers; one has come to predict fun walks, the other potential pain. Learning by consequence is responsible for a dog's choice to either sit politely for what he wants or to bark until you give it over; each dog will use the behaviors that have proven successful in the past.

Let's take a closer look at these ways of learning, and how to make the most of them as a dog walker.

Classical conditioning, or learning by association

We learn by association
I mentioned that all learning organisms learn in these two ways, and that includes us. We make associations all the time, arriving at

positive, negative, or neutral feelings about things, situations, places, people, experiences. You've probably met people you've taken an instant dislike to, and a few you've bonded with very quickly. Imagine you've met one of each at a dinner party last night. Today while pushing a full cart through the grocery store you turn the corner to find the former coming toward you. Your stomach turns over as you wonder, "Has he seen me? Is it too late?" You consider ditching your cart and eating take-out for the week. You've formed a negative association with this person. But what if it's the other person, the one you had a wonderful conversation and exchanged numbers with last night? You have a positive association with this person, and should she be waiting around the corner, you might feel your heart leap instead of your stomach plummet.

Learning by association is emotional learning. We form feelings about things—positive, negative, or neutral—based on our experiences of them.

Dogs learn by association, too

Dogs learn this way, too. This emotional learning is a huge part of how dogs experience the world. Dogs make positive associations (safe or good for me), negative associations (dangerous or bad for me), and neutral associations (no consequence for me) constantly, and these emotional conclusions then shape much of the behavior we see—how dogs respond to various situations, objects, people, and places.

The way dogs react to the sight of a leash is a perfect example. Pull out a leash and the typical dog will go into paroxysms of joy. Why? It's just a length of nylon or leather. But that length of nylon predicts a walk, and walks are fun. Dogs associate leashes with walks and their jumping and wagging results from this positive association. Dogs react similarly, for the same reason, to seeing their dog walker's vehicle pull up outside, and to their dog walker. We predict fun.

The difference between us and dogs

Though we both learn by classical association, dogs and humans are not the same. Understanding how we're different is critical to understanding and working successfully with dogs. Unlike dogs, we humans can intellectualize our feelings, we can think about them. We can step back from a situation (like the chance supermarket encounter) and analyze our emotional response. We can sometimes even talk ourselves out of or down from an emotional reaction. I can say to myself, "Gee, I'm feeling really anxious. I wonder why I'm reacting this strongly? Does this person remind me of something or someone unpleasant? Is my reaction fair or reasonable?" If I decide my reaction isn't rational, I can take a breath and choose not to act on how I feel.

We humans can have a meta-level conversation with ourselves about what we're feeling. Dogs cannot do this. Dogs form positive, negative, and neutral associations—but no thinking goes along with them. Dogs can't rationalize or analyze what they feel, and they can't control their feelings. Reflecting on an emotional reaction is a human talent. Dogs just have the reaction.

Why learning by association matters to dog walkers

Dogs' inability to think about or control their emotional responses means dog behavior isn't always going to be rational. (Not that ours is, but we can sometimes rise to the occasion.) But it also means dogs' emotional associations can be manipulated—something we can take good advantage of. The associations dogs make affect their behavior. A dog afraid of people may bark or growl in the hope of making a stranger move farther away. A dog who likes people is more likely to wag and lick than bark or growl—definitely preferable behavior. Part of our job is to help dogs make positive associations with the things we need them to like—us, their walking route, strangers passing by, other dogs on leash, etc.

The first step is understanding that our own behavior as dog walkers can affect the associations dogs make. Let's start with an example out of context: imagine we're in a sterile laboratory room with only a simple folding chair sitting in the middle. We bring a dog in to explore. The dog is likely to form a neutral association with the chair—nothing good or bad about it. Our assignment is to create a positive association with the chair, so we lower an opaque screen between it and the dog. We periodically raise the screen and each time the dog sees the chair little bits of cheese appear from a dispenser. When the screen lowers the cheese-dispensing stops. If the screen is raised and there's no chair, there's no cheese. We repeat this exercise a few times and before we know it, the dog's association has shifted from neutral to positive: each time he sees the chair, he wags his tail and salivates in anticipation of cheese.

You've probably encountered this type of experiment in high school science class studying Pavlov's dogs. Pavlov coined the term "classical conditioning," which is sometimes also called Pavlovian conditioning. And though usually associated with making a dog anticipate something good, classical conditioning works in both directions: we can also teach the dog to hate or fear the same chair by associating it with something painful or frightening. Instead of cheese each time the screen rises to reveal the chair, we can set off a loud noise or press the button on an e-collar remote control. It wouldn't take long for our subject to decide the chair was unsafe and, depending on his temperament, either roll on his back and whimper in fear, or bark and growl at the scary chair.

This is a silly example, of course. But it illustrates the control we have over the associations dogs make. With this story in mind, let's imagine I'm walking a dog for the first time. Everything is going well until we see another dog across the street. My girl begins yipping and whining and pulling. She's excited and would like to go say hi, but she's making an almighty racket. It's embarrassing or maybe it startles me, so I tell her, sternly, "No!" and give her a leash correction. Startled by the pain, she stops. We move on. The scenario repeats itself over the next few weeks each time we encounter a dog. I'm frustrated—didn't I already tell her, multiple times, to stop that behavior? So I increase the force of my correction. She stops for the moment each time, but the behavior itself continues. Eventually, though, I notice her response to seeing other dogs is changing; she starts turning her head away or stalling or even lying down and rolling over at the site of another dog. Or perhaps her excited yipping and pulling switches to deep-throated woo-woo-woo barking and lunging. What in the world is going on?

I thought I was communicating, "I don't like that response. Don't do that!" And I felt justified in increasing the punishment because I'd had to repeat myself multiple times. But what happened for the dog was simple classical conditioning, or learning by association. What I was actually teaching wasn't "Stop yipping and whining; it embarrasses me." It was "Dogs equal pain." Every time my dog saw another dog, she experienced a leash correction and my anger with her. With enough repetition, that one-on-one connection began to influence how my dog felt about other dogs. Dogs' minds are much simpler than ours; whatever they're engaged with when something good or bad happens is what they associate with the good thing or the bad thing. So while I thought I was communicating, "Please don't do that, you're embarrassing me," my dog experienced, "Seeing other dogs means my walker gets really mad at me." Over time, this changed how she felt about seeing other dogs while out on a leash walk, which resulted in a very different behavior change from what I was after.

Why we use positive training methods

In short, it's easy to fall into these interspecies miscommunications. We think we're saying one thing; the dogs are experiencing something else. This is one reason why all the training strategies you'll learn in this book are positive. We're far less likely to inadvertently create negative associations using positive methods.

If you've been involved in the dog industry for any amount of time you know there's a great deal of controversy surrounding dog training methodology. (Have you ever heard the quip, "The only thing two dog trainers agree on is what the third dog trainer is doing wrong"?) Here's what's important to know:

First of all, the science is in, and it has been for years. A lot of the conversation about methodology is outdated; the research makes it clear we're no longer in a place historically where all opinions on this subject have equal value.

But any positive reinforcement dog trainer who tries to tell you that punishment doesn't work is being disingenuous. That's simply not true. The science is very clear on this, too. Of course punishment works; anything that changes behavior works, and pain and fear change behavior. But using pain and fear risks behavioral side effects from classical conditioning, such as in my example of (quite accidentally) turning a social dog into one who's fearful or upset when she encounters other dogs on leash. Or imagine a dog who's a resource guarder. A traditional trainer will use punishment to teach the dog to stop growling at people approaching his food bowl. If the trainer is good, the dog will stop growling. But he's still upset about being approached, and having his warning cues punished out makes the dog much more dangerous; I'm likely to walk right on up while he's eating, thinking all is okay. A positive-based trainer will instead work to change the underlying emotions that fuel the guarding. She'll use a series of exercises to teach the dog that it's actually great to share her food bowl with people. If the trainer is good, the dog will stop growling because she no longer has anything to growl about. This dog is much safer to be around—and happier, too.

Here are two more reasons to use positive methods as a dog walker and avoid techniques that rely on aversives such as pain, fear, or startling: you will be caring for other peoples' animals away from their supervision. There are serious ethical issues around the use of punishment in such a situation. With the movement in our society toward viewing dogs as family members, sometimes even "children," this is an issue that can easily flare tempers. Finally, here's the simplest reason of all: we can train a dog to do anything we need him to do, and teach him to stop doing anything we don't like, very effectively with humane, positive methods. Given this, it becomes difficult to argue for using pain and fear as teaching tools.

Operant conditioning, or learning by consequence

We learn by consequence
Learning by consequence is about payoff. It's about getting what we want and avoiding things we don't like. People work for money; the consequence of sitting behind a desk in a cubicle for 40 hours a week is a paycheck. (Aren't you glad you chose a different line of work?) Children whine because it often gets them what they want. But a child is less likely to whine if she's sent to her room each time she tries it. We learn to do what works and to avoid what doesn't.

Dogs learn by consequence, too
Dogs are good at learning by consequence. They quickly figure out who's worth begging from. They learn whether it's a sit or a bark that will get you to open the door for them. They learn that pulling on leash works to get them where they want to go. They learn that coming when called is worthwhile during a walk (when it means a treat and being told to "go play") but that coming at the end of a walk is to be avoided if at all possible (when it means being leashed up and taken home).

The difference between us and dogs
Dogs understand the cause-and-effect relationship behind learning by consequence: if I do this, that happens. But they only understand the relationship in real time. I can tell a school-age child I'll take him out for ice cream when I see him next week to celebrate the good report card he received today. When he eats the ice cream, he'll

understand he's being rewarded for grades he got a week ago, which he earned because of work he did over several months. A dog could never understand this—it's way beyond his ability to connect events. Dogs learn by consequence like we do, but only if the consequence is immediate; it must occur right on the heels of the action that caused it. You can't say to a dog when you drop him home after a walk, "You behaved so well on our walk today, here's a treat for that. Thank you!" You could do this each day, but the dog will never understand what the treats are for and they will have no impact on his walking behavior. (Other than looking expectantly at you at the end of the walk for a treat he's come to expect due to classical conditioning!)

Why learning by consequence matters to dog walkers

If you want a dog to learn something, your timing matters. Your response to a dog's behavior has to be immediate for the dog to connect the consequence (either positive or negative) to his own behavior. If you're teaching a dog a new behavior, such as recall, you have to be ready to reward the behavior right away. If the dog comes when you call but you're busy and get the treat to him late, he'll learn considerably more slowly and you'll never build the reliable behavior you're after. The same goes for negative consequences—if you call the dog and he doesn't come running, but you're too busy to put him on leash as a time-out for not responding, you undermine the learning process. You can't approach the dog a minute or two later and expect him to understand why he's been put on leash.

Learning by consequence also matters to dog walkers because reinforced behaviors will increase, and ignored ones will decrease (unless the behavior is self-reinforcing, in which case a time-out or another form of reward removal is needed). Paying attention to what you reward or reinforce—both intentionally and inadvertently—means getting more canine behavior you like, and less you don't.

If a dog drops a ball at your feet and barks at you, throwing the ball tells her that barking works, and you'll likely find her barking at you again once she's retrieved her ball. On the other hand, if you walk away or even pick up and pocket the ball, the dog will eventually learn that barking is not the proper way to ask to have her ball thrown, and she'll try something else—a sit or a quiet stare, perhaps. If you throw her ball only when she's quiet, you'll get more quiet. She'll learn that barking doesn't work for you and if, like me, barking isn't one of your favorite things about dogs, you'll probably enjoy walking her quite a bit more.

Jumping is another great example. Dog walkers get jumped on a lot. Dogs are pretty happy to see you when you arrive at their homes, and jumping is one way they show their excitement. If you reward a dog for jumping on you (however unintentionally) by clipping on his leash and taking him for a walk, you'll continue to be jumped on every day. If instead you step back outside as soon as a dog's front feet leave the floor, every time, the dog will learn to keep all four on the floor. He's very motivated to figure out what's making you leave—he wants his walk, after all. Here's the training sequence (be sure to build in extra time to your pick up schedule for a week or so while the dog works out the training puzzle):

1. Walk through the door. If the dog jumps on you, turn around and leave.

2. Wait outside the door for 30-60 seconds, then repeat Step 1 until the dog doesn't jump on you.

3. Reach down to pet the dog. If the dog jumps on you, turn around and leave.

4. Continue this sequence until you can walk through the door, say hello to the dog, calmly put on his collar and leash, and walk out, all without being jumped on.

Dog walking would be a lot easier if dogs spoke English. You could just walk in and say, "Hey, if you don't jump on me, I'll take you for a walk right now." Or, "Tell you what: if you sit quietly, I'll throw your ball." Or, "Hey, it's kind of obnoxious when you bark at dogs you want to say hi to. Would you mind cutting that out?" But since dogs don't speak our language, we have to rely on an understanding of learning theory to clearly and patiently show dogs which behaviors we'd like to see more of, and which we'd prefer they drop from their repertoire.

The learning theory quadrants

One of the hardest things about learning theory is the anti-intuitive language. As you look at the chart below, keep in mind that "positive" in this context doesn't necessarily mean good—it implies the *addition* of something (good or bad). And "negative" doesn't necessarily mean bad—it implies the *removal* of something (good or bad). Also, the words "reinforcement" and "punishment" have very specific meanings in learning theory, too— reinforcement refers to the attempt to increase a wanted behavior, while punishment refers to the attempt to decrease an unwanted one.

Positive Reinforcement Add something good to increase behavior Ex: Give treats for lying down, and the dog lies down more frequently	Negative Punishment Remove something good to decrease behavior Ex: Pocket the ball when a dog barks at you to throw it, and barking for fetch decreases
Positive Punishment Add something bad to decrease behavior Ex: Shock a dog for humping, and the dog's humping decreases	Negative Reinforcement Remove something bad to increase behavior Ex: Tell a dog to sit and shock him until he does, and the dog's sitting increases

We advocate only the use of the top two quadrants: positive reinforcement and negative punishment. To avoid the confusion the language causes, we call negative punishment "reward removal," as the idea is to give the dog a negative consequence by removing something he likes. A time-out is a common example of reward removal.

Here's one more look at the four quadrants in action using the example of teaching a dog not to jump up on you:

1. Positive reinforcement: pet the dog and leash her up for a walk when she's not jumping.

2. Negative punishment: turn around and walk away when she does jump on you.

3. Positive punishment: knee the dog in the chest and/or yell at her when she jumps on you.

4. Negative reinforcement: pinch the dog's ear until she puts her paws back on the floor.

Again, we advocate only the use of the first two methods—often, as in the case of jumping, in conjunction with each other.

Canine myth busting: right vs. wrong

Classical and operant conditioning together govern both the canine world view and canine behavior. Learning by association teaches dogs what is safe for them and what is dangerous. A small dog who enjoys positive encounters with big dogs "learns" that big dogs are "safe." A small dog who's overwhelmed by an experience or two with a larger dog may come to the opposite conclusion. The first dog is likely to be friendly toward dogs bigger than her. The second may hide or even bark and growl at large dogs. And learning by consequence teaches dogs what works for them and what doesn't. Many dogs learn that it's worth begging food from people, but worthless trying to get the refrigerator to feed them, even though they know that big, shiny box holds all the good stuff. And dogs will learn it works to bark at Dad to throw the ball, but that Mom never falls for that—so Dad gets barked at a lot and Mom doesn't.

Dogs are motivated to do what works for them, and to avoid what doesn't. They're motivated to do things that are safe, and to avoid things that aren't. But they don't understand right from wrong. They *can't* understand right from wrong. Right versus wrong is a human construct that even we humans don't grasp until we reach a certain developmental stage. Animals don't share an ethical world view with us. They don't choose to do things because they're right, or avoid behaviors because they're wrong. They do what works and what's safe; they are amoral. Dogs bark when barking gets them what they want. They jump when jumping works. They don't do any of the things they do in order to annoy us or get back at us, or out of stubbornness.

I can hear the "Yeah, but…" coming. When I taught dog training classes many years ago at the San Francisco SPCA, I never got through this portion of the orientation talk without a "Yeah, but…" so I'm pretty practiced at this part. I know the example you're going to present: "Yeah, but what about when my dog has had an accident in the house? He acts super guilty when I get home, so I know he knows he wasn't supposed to go in the house. I know he knows it was wrong." Let me tell you an alternate version of this story:

A dog gets adopted and moves into a new home. The owners go to work every day, leaving him home to his own devices. He needs to go to the bathroom. The thick rug seems like as good a place as any; in fact, it's quite absorbent. He goes. He feels relieved. He takes a nap. A few hours later he feels the need again, so he goes again. He feels relieved again. Peeing on the rug works, and it's safe. Except that when the owners get home and catch him in the act of peeing a third time, he gets punished—yelled at, possibly swatted on the behind, sent outside. His people think they're teaching him that he's only to go outside. But he doesn't learn the inside/outside rule from this experience. He learns that it's safe to pee on the rug when the people aren't around, but not when they are. So the housetraining problems continue. (If he's a smart dog, he'll probably start peeing on the rug behind the couch, to make sure he's not caught in the act again!) The people come home each day to find an accident in the house and so they punish the dog, who has no idea why he's being punished. He relieved himself hours ago, and we know that cause and effect has to be immediate for a dog to understand it. So his people think they're communicating, "Hey, I thought I told you not to go in the house," and the poor dog has no idea what message he's missing.

Shift forward a few days. The owners come home to a dog looking very "guilty." They realize the dog must have had another accident. They go looking for it and, sure enough, there it is. They assume the guilty looks are the dog admitting that he does, yes, understand that he wasn't supposed to go in the house, so they feel justified in punishing him again. Problem is, the dog isn't feeling guilty. The things his people are reading as guilt—rolling over, looking anxious, tucking his tail between his legs, slinking around or getting low to the ground, licking his lips—these are all appeasement or cut-off signals. These are body language signals dogs use with each other to stop aggression. (You'll learn more about these signals in the next chapter.) He's throwing cut-off signals because he's come to learn, through association, that his people coming home means it's time to be punished. He's noticed the pattern. He doesn't know why he's being aggressed upon, but he's hoping to stop it by sending all the right signals—signals that his people misread as an admission of guilt. What we have here is a tragic interspecies miscommunication.

We assume that because we feel guilt, other animals do, too. We assume that because we know right from wrong, other animals do, too. We assume that because we understand each other when we talk, that dogs get it, too. We know on an intellectual level that they don't understand English, but we still seem flummoxed when they don't understand us. This insistence on reading and treating dogs as though they were furry humans gets us in a lot of trouble.

What letting this myth go does for dog walkers
Letting go of the right versus wrong myth makes working with dogs less confrontational. Instead of assuming a dog is being stubborn about pulling on leash, for example, we can just admit we haven't trained him well enough, and then get on with the business of fixing that. Because dogs don't pull to annoy their dog walkers, they pull to get to something interesting—a place, a smell, a dog walking up the block a ways. If pulling works, they'll keep doing it. Simple as that. If you want them to stop pulling, you have to use training methods that teach them it no longer works—like stopping each time they pull, or even turning to go in the opposite direction. (See Chapter 7 for more details.)

Letting go of the right versus wrong myth makes us better dog walkers. Instead of thinking, "Ugh! I've told him not to do X a thousand times! Why is he being so stubborn / naughty / willful / etc.," you're able to think in terms of problem solving: "He's doing X. I want him to do Y. What's my training plan for getting him there?" This way of thinking—a positive trainer's way of thinking—means better results faster, less frustration, and a more enjoyable relationship with the dogs in your care.

Canine myth busting: dominance and submission
A lot of the conventional training wisdom floating around our culture is based on the idea that dogs arrange themselves in dominance hierarchies, constantly vying to get and keep the top dog position. We're told that we must be the alpha, that we must be ever-vigilant to thwart our dogs' attempts to dominate us, too. Much of the force-based training methods are based on this view of dogs, which evolved from a famous wolf research study. Problem is, dogs aren't wolves.

(Also, we're not dogs, and our dogs know that.) There's an additional problem as well—the wolf research has been greatly misunderstood. In fact, the original researchers themselves have cried foul over the misuse of their work as the basis of this pervasive misunderstanding of canine social interactions and the justification for use of force-based methods.

The key to understanding dogs' social interactions is to view them in context. Imagine you've taken over a group of three dogs from another walker. You throw a tennis ball for them and watch as Barney snarks the other two dogs off the ball. If you didn't know better, you might assume Barney is the dominant dog in this pack. A bit later you set down a water bowl. All three noses go for the water, but Spot growls her compatriots off. She drinks her fill and then the other two companionably share what's left. You wonder if perhaps you got it wrong—it must be Spot who's in charge. But when you accidentally drop a treat on the ground and Fido lets Barney and Spot know with a nice display of snarling that the treat is all hers, you find yourself befuddled. Who is alpha in this group after all?

No one is alpha—that's the point. Social hierarchy is contextual and in constant motion because it's all about resources, and who wants what most at any given moment. All three dogs would have liked to have retrieved the ball. But Barney wanted it most. When he snarked, the other two dogs essentially said, "Hey, if you want it that bad, fine. I don't want it enough to bother fighting over it." Similarly, all three dogs were thirsty, but Barney and Fido acquiesced to let Spot have her drink first. She seemed to want it more, and the others didn't deem it worth fighting for. But though Fido was willing to back down about the ball and water, she felt very strongly about that treat and let her companions know it. Wisely, they let her have it. So Barney is in charge of balls, Spot rules the water dish, and Fido gets any free treats that happen to fall to the ground. At least in this moment. Should Barney or Fido feel particularly parched one day, they may challenge Spot for first water dibs. You might see some good growling and such as they communicate to decide who wants the water more in that moment.

The point is that it's all about resources and context, not about temperament. Some dogs have more confident personalities than others, sure. But that isn't the same as claiming that dogs form hierarchical packs and spend their time constantly trying to get the upper hand on each other and on us.

The damage this myth does

Insisting on labeling dogs as "dominant" or "submissive" gets us dog pros in a lot of trouble. First, calling a dog dominant doesn't really mean much, and can bring us into conflict with clients. We all have different views of the term dominant. Tell one owner her dog is dominant, and she may glow with pride. Tell another and she may wring her hands in worry and fear. Tell a third and she may become angry with you. And the term doesn't carry any useful information. If I say a dog is dominant, what does it mean? You don't know, because you don't know what behavior I've observed that's led me to label the dog thus. You don't know whether I consider it a good trait or a bad one. And if I consider dominance a problem, my labeling the dog leads to all sorts of counter-productive behavior on my part. I may feel compelled to assert my dominance over the dog, following dangerous advice such as alpha rolling (the best possible way to get bitten in the face), or silly advice such as worrying over not allowing the dog to cross a threshold in front of me.

What letting this myth go does for dog walkers

It's much more constructive to take leave of labels and simply state specifically what the dog is doing or not doing that concerns you. Take Barney, for example. We could label him dominant because he doesn't like to share tennis balls. Or we could simply state: "When I throw a tennis ball and other dogs try to chase it, Barney snarks at them." Now we're getting somewhere. Once I describe the behavior, it's simply a matter of deciding what I want to do about it. I can decide it's not a problem and leave it alone. I can decide to remove balls from the group. Or I can decide to help Barney learn to share. In other words, I can formulate a productive plan. And by doing so, I avoid unnecessary power struggles with an animal who has teeth, and avoid misunderstandings with or potentially offending Barney's people.

It's a tall order, letting go of such a pervasive cultural belief. But I encourage you to try hard to avoid the use of labeling terms for dogs in favor of specific descriptions of behavior that lead to formulating a positive training plan. You and the dogs in your care will both be happier. I've included some great additional reading on this subject in the Resources section of the book if you'd like to explore the topic further. And the next chapters on canine body language and aggression should shed further light as well.

Chapter 3

Reading Dog Body Language

There are entire books written on the body language of dogs, and for good reason. Few things are more important to a dog pro than a keen and thorough understanding of canine body language, and yet it's an area we rarely study well. We tend to rely on our instincts to guide us, interpreting dog behavior through our human eyes. We assume a dog yawn means the same as a human one, that a guilty look and posture means guilt, that rolling over surely must be an invitation for a good belly rub. Unfortunately we're often wrong, and rarely realize our mistakes. In our self-centered hubris we fail to remember dogs are not humans. We take action based on our erroneous assumptions and then wonder where things went wrong: why did the dog bite? Why does he keep doing things when he clearly knows he's not supposed to?

Serious dog professionals eventually learn to stop reading the dog as a human and read the dog as a dog. That's one of the things that separates us from the average dog lover. This chapter won't teach you everything you should know about how dogs communicate. As I mentioned, there are whole books on that subject. This chapter will give you a framework and general pointers for understanding dog body language. Then, in the Resources section at the back of this book, you'll find recommended books and DVDs to continue your study of this fascinating and misunderstood language.

Why you need to understand "dog"

To avoid dog-dog conflicts
Most dog-dog scuffles and fights are easily avoided by recognizing early warning signs that conflict is brewing. When you know what you're watching for, you can step in and redirect the dogs onto some-

thing else before trouble erupts—much like a kindergarten teacher or parent might do when they notice two children heading toward a squabble. If you find yourself scratching your head when dogs have an argument, wondering where it came from, you're likely missing a rich assortment of signals ahead of time. Fights rarely erupt out of nowhere; there's almost always time to head them off if you're "listening."

To avoid dog-human conflicts

The same goes with dog-human conflicts, whether between your charges and a stranger or between them and yourself. Most bites to humans are fully avoidable. We get bitten because we don't "listen" when dogs tell us they're uncomfortable, would prefer not to be touched, are frightened, etc. We fail to read their body language signals, forcing them to go bigger with growls, barks, lunges, snaps, or, if we really push, a bite. And often we punish them for giving us warning signals like growling and snarling—we punish them for communicating. I always thank a dog who growls at me, I thank them for letting me know. I know he won't understand what I'm saying, but it reminds me to keep perspective. A dog who growls makes a decision; he could have just bitten. I'm grateful to be warned off. But I also try to keep these moments to a minimum—if I'm paying good attention to the subtler body language I'm less likely to be growled at in the first place.

To keep Fido happy

We choose to work with dogs for a living because we care deeply for them. Reading body language allows us to notice when something is amiss, when a dog is nervous or scared or upset. We're able to see the signs early then look for cues in the environment to figure out what's causing the discomfort so we can take action before things get worse, and can make sure the dogs we care for are having a great time. I've seen many a situation in which a dog walker didn't realize a dog in her care was struggling. For example, I worked with a walker who was perplexed by a dog's refusal to get into her vehicle and was becoming frustrated with the dog. But if she'd been reading the dog's body language, she'd have understood he was anxious—and if she'd looked back at the dog already in her car and read his language, she'd have understood why: the dog she was picking up first was giving the second one clear signals to stay out of the vehicle. Instead, the walker physically forced the dog into her car each day and then didn't understand why the dog eventually started balking at even having his leash put on when she came to pick him up. You know something's wrong when a dog isn't excited to see his walker!

To communicate more effectively

It's a tricky thing to live and work with a different species. Dogs' ability to understand us is limited (though you have to give them kudos for how hard they try!); it's really our responsibility to close the communication gap. The more you understand what dogs are saying and how to communicate better with them, the better able you are to get your job done and enjoy the incredible work of being a dog walker.

How dogs communicate

Dogs communicate in three ways: through scent, through body language, and verbally. Unfortunately for us humans, verbal communication is their weakest point and the one they rely on least, while scent—a communication channel we use mostly subconsciously and lack the biology to master—is their strongest and most salient. Fortunately, dogs are masters of body language, and their wide array of signals is something you can learn, if you're willing.

The first thing to understand about dog body language is that it's ritualized. That is, dogs use a collection of deliberate signals with specific intent to communicate. The primary goal is to avoid conflict and gain cooperation. This makes good evolutionary sense, as dogs are well equipped to do damage to each other. The goal of evolution is to pass on one's genes, which is hard to do if you keep getting in fights and end up critically wounded.

When things go wrong

Over the course of your career with dogs, you'll come across some who just don't get along with other dogs. The aggression chapter will cover various dog-dog issues, from leash reactivity to compulsive fighting. But why do these kinds of problems happen?

Dogs come into the world with innate behaviors designed to help them navigate life among their own, and then continue to learn appropriate conflict-avoidance behavior as puppies in a litter and then out and about in the world. In short, their behavior—like our own—is a mixture of genes and socialization. Tragic breakdowns can occur in both parts of the equation.

It's an unfortunate practice among some breeders—both professional and accidental—to breed dogs with poor temperaments. If you breed an aggressive dog, it should be no surprise when the puppies grow into aggressive dogs. Placing equal selective emphasis on personality and physical characteristics would go a long way toward ending aggression in pet dogs.

But socialization also plays its part. It's critical that puppies be raised in the presence of other puppies and dogs so they learn appropriate behavior and are comfortable with their own kind. The misguided practice of keeping dogs indoors and away from other dogs and people until they've had their full set of shots has filled our shelters to overflowing. The key socialization window for puppies begins to close at 16 weeks of age. After this time their ability to comfortably assimilate new experiences diminishes quickly. Keeping dogs away from others during this period is similar to keeping a child locked away until the age of five and then expecting her to be able to assume normal interactions with other children. While parvovirus is a devastating disease, its prevalence is greatly exaggerated. Far more dogs die each year in shelters due to behavior issues directly attributable to poor socialization than ever contract parvo. (For more information on this issue, read AVSAB's statement on parvo and socialization and visit the Operation Socialization website. You'll find the URLs for both in the Resources section.)

Key tips for reading body language

Read the entire dog
Conventional wisdom tends to place too much emphasis on single signals. For example, we're told to watch a dog's tail—everything's okay if it's wagging. But that's not necessarily true. Dogs use their entire bodies to communicate. Reading only the tail is like talking to someone on a cell phone when it's cutting in and out. Tails wag in many ways, and what the rest of the body is doing while the tail is wagging is just as important.

Read the dog in context
A story without a setting isn't much of a story. When you're reading a dog, pay attention to the setting, to the surrounding environment. What's going on? Are there other dogs present? Are they familiar or new? Are there other distractions, good or bad? A cat or squirrel you hadn't noticed, or a person giving off strange vibes? Maybe a loud or

startling noise? Much of your job is to read comfort and discomfort so you can step in early to avoid unnecessary incidents and make sure the dogs are having a great time. Body language communicates a dog's internal state, and the environment impacts that.

Read the other dog(s)

Dog professionals learn to watch the entire interaction between dogs—which means watching both or all dogs involved in a situation. To watch just one dog is like listening to someone talking to someone else on a phone—you only get one side of the conversation, and it's easy to get the gist wrong. Often, taking a look at the other dog will give you strong clues about what the dog you're interested in is saying. For example, imagine you're struggling to read a particular set of signals—is he or isn't he comfortable with another dog? You look at the other dog and see that he's backing away slowly—there's your answer. Clearly the first dogs is sending some sort of warning signals; now you just have to look closer to see what they are.

Body language signals

Body language signals fall into four main categories: calming or cut-off signals, fear signals, warning signals, and play signals. These categories and which specific signals fall under them are explained below. You'll notice that some signals appear on more than one list. Just as a human smile can mean many things—joy, embarrassment, irony—so can many canine signals. And thus the tips above to read the entire dog in the moment's context as well as the dogs around him—it's the combination of signals within a given situation we're looking to decipher.

Calming/appeasement/cut-off signals/stress

These signals, as you can see, come with many names. But whatever you call them, the definition is the same: dogs use these signals to turn off or inhibit aggression in other dogs (they try them with us, too, though we often fail to read them correctly). These signals tell other dogs, essentially, "I'm no threat, and I don't want any trouble." Think of a man putting his hands out in front of him, palms out, while backing away from a bully in a bar who has just challenged him. The message is "You win, you're right, I'm sorry, I don't want any trouble." They are non-threatening gestures meant to keep the peace. Also, these signals often indicate stress in the dog displaying them.

Signals in this category include:

- Lip licking (small flicks of the tongue—if you've never noticed this, keep an eye out—you'll see it all the time)
- Yawning
- Head turns (turning away from the other dog to break eye contact)
- Rolling over or lying down
- "Submissive urination" (an unfortunate moniker, this is when dogs piddle on themselves)
- Blinking
- Curving or arcing around the other dog, rather than walking more directly toward him
- Shaking off
- Moving slowly
- Pausing
- Sniffing (showing a sudden interest in the ground, for example)
- Scratching (taking a break to scratch or chew on oneself)

Some of these, particularly the last two, can also be displacement behaviors—behaviors a dog engages in to take the social pressure off while he decides what to do in an unsure, frustrating, or stressful situation.

Fear signals

This collection of signals generally indicates a state of fear in the dog using them. The more overt signals at the end of the list are often misunderstood as aggression, when they are really an attempt by the frightened dog to create social distance from what he fears by frightening it off.

- Ears held back against the head
- Head dropped
- Weight held on the back legs, crouching down (the dog appears to make himself smaller)
- Whale eye (the eyes appear very large and you can see the whites)

- Hackles raised from shoulder to tail
- Tail low, often tucked under the body (sometimes wagging low)
- Mouth opened wide with teeth showing
- Growling
- Snarling/lip curled
- Snapping (snapping of the teeth without contact)

Warning signals
These are threat signals that, when not read or properly responded to by the other dog (or us, for that matter), can lead to aggression.

- Ears held forward
- Stiff posture
- Flag tail (tail held high and stiff, or wagging very slightly)
- Staring (direct, prolonged eye contact)
- Walking straight toward the other dog
- Weight held on the front paws (the dog appears to make himself bigger)
- Hackles raised
- T position (the dog places his head over the back or neck of the other dog)
- Continued, escalating vocalization (for example, a low growl that grows steadily louder)
- Closed mouth, slowed breathing

Note the last signal, compared with a fearful dog. It's common to misunderstand the fearful dog, with his mouth wide open and showing all his teeth, as being aggressive. He really wants nothing more than for the other dog to just go away. Contrast this with a confident dog ready to aggress if he doesn't get the right calming signals in return—he's likely to have his mouth closed, or perhaps open just enough to show canines.

Understanding hackles
Let's take a moment on hackles, as they are so often misunderstood. Conventional wisdom generally

holds that raised hackles means aggression, but you'll notice that hackles appear on multiple lists above. They can mean many things, and you see them across many contexts. Essentially, hackles are an internal state of arousal of some kind. The only time you're certain not to see them is when a dog is resting or relaxed. Hackles don't mean anything good or bad by themselves; they just mean the dog is aroused or alert in some way—could be that he's excited to have a playmate, or that he's scared, or that he's upset. Hackles are a perfect example of the importance of reading the entire dog and the context he's in.

Play signals

We love to see these. There are few things more joyful—at least to a dog lover—than watching a dog invite another to play. Dogs employ a number of signals to get the game going.

- Play bow (elbows on the floor, rear end up in the air)
- Play paw (raising a front paw from the floor, with or without physically touching the other dog with it)
- Play face (face is relaxed, mouth open and grinning)
- Play ears (ears held high and back; sometimes referred to as "sexy ears")
- Tail wagging (wag is big, loose, and tail is held high)
- Bouncy, inefficient movement (movements are big and exaggerated, even silly)
- Hackles raised

Conflicting signals

These lists are great guidelines, but behavior is far more complex than can ever be captured by a set of lists. What do you make of it, for instance, when a dog shows signals from different lists all at once? How would you interpret a play paw combined with a lip lick and a freeze, for example? When you see signals from multiple lists, you're most likely encountering ambivalence. The dog is conflicted, unsure. In this example, he may want to play but be nervous about it, and has been pushed into discomfort by an enthusiastic response to his initial play signal. We all know the feeling of ambivalence, of being unable to decide between options with the resulting warring emotions. Wanting to kiss someone for the first time, perhaps, but also feeling afraid to do so. When you see a dog showing conflicting signals, it may be best to jump in and help with a little cheerleading and perhaps a recall to give the dog a quick break from the situation so he can better decide what he wants. Ambivalence can easily turn into actual conflict when a dog is pushed too hard.

What to do with the signals

We can step in to help dogs avoid conflict when we understand what we're seeing. We can call a dog out of a situation when he's displaying warning cues, for example, or entice him away with a food lure. We can distract a dog who's overwhelming another, because we notice the second dog's fear or stress. We can cheerlead and encourage a dog using play signals. We can give two dogs a break in play when we start to notice an increase in cut-off signals during play, ensuring that play doesn't tip into conflict. In short, dog walkers are the blacktop monitors of the dog world; our job is to make sure everybody gets along by stepping in before things go too far.

Watch for alerting behavior

Alerting behavior is a particular combination of signals dog walkers should always be on the watch for: ears forward, tail up, body oriented forward toward something that has caught the dog's attention. Alerting sometimes also comes with raised hackles and/or a raised paw. This combination of signals tells you the dog has become aware of and aroused by something—could be a squirrel to chase or another dog to bark at while on leash, for example. This is a great training moment, a chance to redirect the dog's attention to you before he lunges or barks, and to then reward him for doing so. It's much easier to catch the dog before he reacts than to get his attention back—or to literally get him back, if he's off leash. And with repeated practice, he will eventually learn to turn to you in these moments without even being asked.

Chapter 4

Understanding Aggression

Aggression is a widely misunderstood concept. A clean, scientific understanding of aggression is invaluable to professional dog walkers. In short, then, there are three reasons dogs aggress:

1. To resolve conflict over resources

2. In response to fear

3. Hard-wired predatory behavior

1. Aggression to resolve conflict over resources

This is the most common type of aggression you'll encounter as a dog walker. Dogs may fight over food, objects such as tennis balls or sticks, water, breeding access to a female dogs, access to you (as the giver of all things fun and delicious, walkers can become a resource to their dogs), and control of spaces. As discussed in the last chapter, the vast majority of these encounters never move past ritualized posturing behavior.

2. Fear aggression

Dogs may be fearful of other canines or of people (or more specific sub-categories, such as big dogs or men) due to previous bad experiences or, more commonly, because of inadequate socialization as puppies. Dogs who aren't given a wide range of positive experiences with other dogs, people, and life situations outside the home during puppyhood (often due to outmoded advice from veterinarians to keep pups inside until vaccinations are complete) are likely to suffer from the effects of undersocialization—a fear of new experiences or categories of people and dogs they didn't encounter when young. Behavior problems stemming from undersocialization are the number one reason for relinquishment and euthanasia today.[1,2]

Some dogs show their fear by making themselves small, crouching and rolling to expose their bellies. Most fearful dogs will increase distance from the scary thing if they can, by avoidance or outright flight from the scene. But some dogs learn over time that growling or barking or snapping at the scary dog or person often makes him move away. Once a dog is on to this tactic, fear-aggressive displays can become larger and more scary-looking over time.

Though fearful dogs would much rather disengage from what frightens them, they are every bit as much a bite risk if pushed as a dog displaying true aggressive behavior.

3. Predation

True predation. Most of the time the predation category of aggression is simply about feeding oneself. For example, dogs may chase small animals such as squirrels or gophers. This is natural, hard-wired behavior for a predator. We often forget that our four-legged friends have not been domesticated all that long, evolutionarily speaking. If you've ever seen a dog go after a prey animal, you'll notice he gives no ritualized warning. The action is quiet and swift; there's no benefit to letting a potential meal know you're coming.

Compulsive fighting. Compulsive fighters are dogs who will fight any dog on sight, to the death if allowed. This is generally believed to be a result of breeding for fighting dogs. Not only is this practice abhorrent for the dogs involved, some of these dogs' genes find their way back into the general breeding population as well, to tragic effect.

Predatory drift. In predatory drift, the prey instinct is triggered in an inappropriate situation. Dogs are programmed to respond to small, running animals and to high-pitched squeaks—the behaviors elicited by prey animals. Unfortunately, sometimes dogs—and human children—also exhibit these behaviors. It's more common

---

[1]"Reasons for Relinquishment of Companion Animals in U.S. Animal Shelters" by Janet M. Scarlett, et al. in the *Journal of Applied Animal Welfare Science*, 1999.

[2]"Human and Animal Factors Related to the Relinquishment of Dogs and Cats in 12 Selected Animal Shelters in the United States" by M.D. Salman, et al. in the *Journal of Applied Animal Welfare Science*, 1998.

than is generally realized for dogs to kill other dogs (and, more rarely, human children) in predatory drift incidents. For example, for a larger dog to kill a small dog in a daycare, group walk, or even a home setting. Small dogs can look alarmingly like prey animals when they tuck their tails and run, and they are given to nervous squeaks when startled or overwhelmed. These stimuli can kick off predation behavior in other dogs. And a significant size difference can mean serious maiming or death for the smaller dog.

Predatory drift can also be a group phenomenon, as the prey sequence is a group activity among wild dogs. In other words, dogs will sometimes gang up on a running or squealing dog. The most famous incident of this kind was a documented case of a group of beagles that killed one of its own pack members when it became tangled in a fence and began to struggle and squeal in distress.

There are two critical things to understand about predatory drift: dogs who kill other dogs in a predatory drift incident are not aggressive or "bad" dogs. They are not intending to kill one of their own. They may have never shown any signs of aggression toward another dog in the past. They may be among the most friendly and accomplished players. It can happen to any dog. However, dogs with high prey drive (dogs who like to chase things, especially small animals) may be at higher risk.

The second thing to understand is that predatory drift can—and usually does—happen between dogs who know and like each other. As I said, it most commonly happens in daycares, on dog walks, in private homes. Dogs can be best friends but that's no insurance against predatory drift.

The 50% rule

So how do you protect against predatory drift? Follow the 50% rule. Dogs who have more than a 50% weight differential should not play together unsupervised. And even when supervised, they shouldn't engage in chasing and wrestling, as predatory drift happens so swiftly human intervention from even a couple of feet away is usually not fast enough to save the smaller dog.

We recommend dog walkers group dogs by weight, following the 50% rule. So a 30-pound dog might be walked with dogs as small as 15 pounds or as large as 60 pounds. (But you have to choose which, because the 15 pound dogs cannot be walked with those who weigh in at 60 pounds.) Though predatory drift can happen among dogs of the same size, it's far less likely a dog will be killed or maimed before the aggressing dog snaps out of the drift.

Other things you should know about aggression

Aggression creates social distance

Other than in the case of predation, the goal of an aggressive display is generally to manipulate social distance—to get a competitor to move away from a resource such as the water dish, or to get a scary thing such as another dog or a stranger to go away. Most aggression is display; actual fighting is, thankfully, rare. (One way to determine whether a particular encounter is ritualized display versus something more serious is to watch for actual contact, for example one dog pinning another to the ground.)

Aggression is context-specific

We often think in terms of aggressive dogs and non-aggressive dogs, as though aggression were a personality trait. But, other than those dogs bred for compulsive fighting (or unlucky enough to have inherited some of those genes), there really are just dogs. All dogs are capable of aggression, and all dogs will exhibit aggression at some point in their lives, just as all people will get into arguments from time to time. Aggression is well within the normal range of dog behavior (though it can look quite scary to us!), and is all about context.

For example, take Norman. Norman is a pretty easy-going dog. He makes dog friends easily and is just the kind of dog a walker might like to have along in a group. But Norman is obsessed with pine cones. Normally laid-back Norman will make it clear to fellow canines, through all sorts of ritualized body language, including an impressive-sounding growl, that the pine cone is his and his alone. Is Norman aggressive in the negative way we often think of aggression? Nope. He just doesn't want to share his pine cone. If it were a tennis ball he'd be happy to share. Sticks? Water? Treats on the ground? No problem. But pine cones? No way. Interestingly, he doesn't mind if a human takes a pine cone from him. In fact, he's happy to have you do that—you might just throw it for him, after all. Again, Norman's behavior, like all aggression, is context driven.

Or take Katie. She likes dogs, but only when she's off leash. If she sees one of her kind while on a leash walk, she does everything she can to avoid interaction. If she can't get away—for example, if another dog approaches her despite all her attempts via body language to say no—she'll air snap and snarl in an attempt to move the dog away. But let her off leash and new dogs can run up to her with no problem; she's always happy to say hi.

Dog walkers need to be aware of each dog's triggers—those specific things or contexts that make them uncomfortable, fearful, or trigger guarding behavior—so we can watch for and control those situations. Walkers also need to think hard about which of these kinds of situations they feel they can safely control—a topic we'll visit in Chapter 8 when we discuss screening and, for group walkers, pack composition.

Remember to avoid the dominance myth

I addressed this issue at length in Chapter 2. The important thing to remember is that the concepts of dominance and submission aren't useful here. In fact, they often cloud the issue. Would you say Norman's pine cone guarding makes him dominant, even though he'll let a dog take just about anything else from him? Is Katie submissive because of her fear, or dominant because of the snapping and snarling? The answer is: it doesn't matter. Those are subjective terms and, as such, carry too little meaning to be helpful.

Labeling dogs also often leads to counter-productive measures on our part. For example, if I decide Norman is being dominant, I may be tempted to make him submit, forcing him to give up the pine cone to other dogs. Though well-meaning, such an approach is likely to escalate the situation.

What is important is accurately describing what each dog is doing, using truly descriptive language. For example: "When Norman has a pine cone and another dog gets within 10 feet of him, he growls." Describe the behavior and then decide what you will do about it. Not walk in areas with pine cones? Walk him with dogs who respect his pine-cone possessiveness? Hire a trainer to teach him to enjoy sharing pine cones with other dogs? We don't need to label Norman in order to choose a safe and effective solution to the situation.

Preventing and handling dog fights

Honest-to-goodness dog fights that result in real damage are remarkably infrequent. This is mostly due to the ritualized body language discussed in Chapter 3, language geared toward avoiding conflict. Conflict is expensive, evolutionarily speaking. Why waste precious energy reserves on actions that can result in injuries, possibly death? Scuffles among dogs, however, are common. Scuffles are the less-serious spats and conflicts that might result in minor injuries like lost fur (and dignity), scrapes, or even a small puncture wound.

Ideally, you want to avoid both. And being able to predict and prevent fights is the best course of action. It's a lot less stressful to prevent fights than to break them up.

Prediction

Fortunately, you don't need a crystal ball to predict a dog fight. Here's a list of things that often lead to spats between dogs:

- Rough play, particularly when it continues uninterrupted at length.
- Targeting behavior, in which a dog incessantly targets another dog for play even when that dog isn't showing any interest or reciprocating the play behavior.
- Herding behavior.
- Stalking behavior.
- Excessive barking. Some dogs attempt to use barking to engage other dogs in play, but this behavior is often not appreciated.
- Failure to read another dog's cut-off or fear signals.
- Stiff body posture.
- Humping.
- Locked gaze or holding eye contact for long periods of time.
- Growling, especially with escalation. Meaning a growl that starts quietly and builds into a louder and louder growl.
- Baring of teeth.
- The presence of coveted resources, particularly among resource guarders. The desirable objects can be anything from toys and tennis balls to food.

These are things you should keep your eyes peeled for. If you do, you'll be able to prevent fights from happening in the first place.

Prevention

Careful screening and pack composition. One key way to prevent dog fights is to carefully choose the dogs you're going to take out into public situations. This is particularly important when walking dogs in groups, especially if the dogs will be off leash and have the opportunity to interact with unknown dogs. It's so important, in fact, that all of Chapter 8 is dedicated to the topic. For now, suffice it to say you shouldn't be shy about reorganizing groups that have a poor dynamic. Separate resource guarders and dogs whose mismatched play styles make walks more difficult. You may even need to fire dogs who are causing more than their fair share of trouble. While it never feels good in the moment to do so, letting difficult dogs go ultimately makes your job more enjoyable and the daily routine less stressful on the remaining dogs.

Situational awareness. Being aware of the surrounding environment, including teaching yourself to scan for approaching dogs and potential resources (chicken bones, garbage, tennis balls, sticks, drinking puddles, etc.) will help you prevent scuffles among your canine charges.

Avoiding interactions with unknown dogs. The only way to be sure two dogs aren't going to get into a fight is to not allow them to interact. And so even if the dogs you're walking are approaching another dog giving all the right body language signals and the unknown dog looks downright friendly and receptive, you're better off calling your dogs cheerfully to you and moving on. In most cases, the dogs would have greeted each other appropriately and would possibly even have had a nice play session. But the more conservative you are, the fewer scuffles you'll see.

Remember you're walking other people's dogs and your job is to keep them safe, not provide them with scores of new canine friends. So whether you're walking a group of dogs off leash or a single dog on leash, keep interactions limited to those between you and the dog(s) or between the dogs in the group.

Active management
Active management means you, the dog pro, being in the game, focused on the dogs in your care and managing the environment to the best of your ability to set your dogs up for success and keep them safe.

Establish the tone. By asking for some simple obedience behaviors at the outset of the walk to focus the dogs on you and requiring them to calm down and pay attention, you set the tone for the walk.

Build strong recalls. Strong recalls allow you to call dogs away from unknown dogs, potentially desirable resources, and out of amped up play before it tips over into argument.

Reward off-leash dogs for checking in. The closer your dogs are to you, the easier it is to monitor their behavior and keep them out of trouble.

Take frequent obedience breaks. Stop now and then to practice sits or touches or recalls so you can use these exercises to interrupt play sessions. Dogs are like kids in this respect. The longer the play continues, the more likely it is an argument breaks out. By calling dogs out of play every one to two minutes to practice a couple of obedience behaviors, give them a treat, and let them return to play, you keep the game from becoming too intense. Over time this routine teaches the dogs to self-regulate—dog walkers who consistently apply obedience breaks will notice the dogs begin to take play breaks on their own to check in with their walker for treats.

Apply time-outs for bullying, repeated harassment, excessive chasing, excessive barking, and humping. These behaviors often lead to scuffles, and consistent use of time-outs helps dogs learn more appropriate ways of playing with their buddies. Time-outs are discussed in more detail in Chapter 5.

Redirect dogs with difficult play styles to toys, more appropriate playmates, or other pursuits.

Interrupt stalking and herding behaviors by calling dogs to you and rewarding them for walking alongside you.

Interrupt before fights happen. Anytime you see anything you recognize as a predictor of a fight, whether it's excessive chasing, two dogs circling each other with stiff body posture, or two dogs staring each other down, don't wait to see if a conflict erupts. Proactively step in by cheerfully calling the dogs to you and redirecting their attention onto something else.

Breaking up fights

Again, prevention is always better. But when the worst happens, the first thing to remember is: Never grab a dog's collar. You are likely to make the situation worse by heightening the tension and removing flight from the fight-or-flight menu. It's also an excellent way to get bitten, as it's common for dogs in the midst of a fight to turn and redirect their bite onto the person who grabbed their collar.

Instead of touching either dog, attempt to break up the fight by startling the dogs. By far the best way to do this is using a startling sound. A sharp hand clap can work in small scuffles. For more serious dog fights, you'll need something much louder, like an air horn. You can buy air horns at party stores. If you carry an air horn, remember it will be of more use to you if it's attached to your belt or in another easy and quick-to-grab location. An air horn at the bottom of a backpack does you no good when fur is flying.

Another option is spraying the dogs with water, such as squirting them in the face with your water bottle. If you have neither noise nor water, you can try tossing an article of clothing like your jacket over their heads or using citronella or pepper spray. We don't generally recommend the latter as a first recourse, as these irritants can get in the eyes of both the aggressor and the aggressed-upon, as well as the eyes of other dogs in the area and yours.

If it's absolutely necessary to remove the dogs from each other with physical force, your best option is to grab the dog who appears to be the aggressor by the tail or hind legs and lift swiftly backward and up into the air. But please note that you do risk being bitten by taking this course of action.

Fortunately, the vast majority of dog fights are easily broken up with a loud noise.

After a fight

Once the dogs are separated, immediately step in to keep them apart and occupy them with other things. Don't let them interact again that day. Put the aggressor on leash if he isn't already, and if it was more than a mild scuffle, take the dogs home.

Adrenaline continues to be produced in a dog's body for 10 to 15 minutes after a fight is over and it can take the body three to six days to reabsorb these stress hormones, depending on how agitated the dog was. For this reason, it's best to leave dogs who have been in a fight home for a day or two, as they will be more likely than usual to get into new scuffles until their adrenaline levels drop again.

Chapter 5

Pack Management

Whether you're walking single dogs or groups, on or off leash, how you manage your charges matters. Pack management is about keeping the dogs, yourself, and others safe, about liability protection, about making a good impression for your business and the profession of dog walking, and about you and the dogs having the best time possible each and every outing.

Setting the tone

A tone will be set for your walk whether you set it or not, so it's best to address this proactively. Ideally, you want the tone to be calm, cheerful, and focused. Leave tone setting up to most dogs and it will be frantic, cheerful, and zany. This can make for an exhausting and frustrating day. So take control.

Tone setting starts before you even open a dog's front door. Is he barking in excitement that you're there? Wait it out. Remember from the learning theory in Chapter 1 that dogs do what works. If you teach the dogs you walk to bark at you to open the door, that's what they'll do. If you teach them instead that they must calm down first, you'll get a quiet greeting.

Now it's time to open the door and step inside. Does the dog jump on you? You can hardly blame him—he thinks you're the bee's knees and he's terribly excited to see you. But if you don't enjoy being pummeled by paws and want a calm, controlled walk, leave and close the door. Yep, leave. Stand outside for 20 or 30 seconds, then try again. The minute a dog's paws leave the floor, you're on your way out again. You aren't angry; no need to yell or tell him he's a bad dog. You're just calmly teaching him that jumping on you doesn't get him the results he wants. Four on the floor? That's more like it—you're happy to leash him up when he's calm. You can even, once you've got the jumping under control, begin requiring a sit as a prerequisite for leashing him up to go.

Consistency is everything

Remember consistency is everything when we're dealing with operant conditioning, or learning by consequence. Once you begin teaching a dog, for example, that it's not okay to jump on you, it must never again be okay to jump on you. If you make the mistake of allowing the jumping on a day when you're feeling rushed, you won't set the training back by a little bit. You'll reset it entirely. It's critical the dog learns jumping *never* works. If he thinks it might still work sometimes, he'll keep trying it. He's not being naughty; he's just doing what seems to work, particularly because jumping is easier and more fun than not jumping.

Leash manners are part of tone setting, too. Allowing a dog to drag you down the driveway to your car or the sidewalk will set the tone for the rest of the walk. Insist that Fido walk calmly from the first second you hit the front stoop or apartment hall. See Chapter 7 for tips on how to teach dogs to walk nicely on leash.

If you're transporting dogs to another location for the walk, tone setting continues in the car. Ask dogs to sit and wait before being invited to jump into your vehicle. They should also sit and wait for your cue to jump back out once you've reached the walking destination. This is a good safety measure, too, as it prevents a dog from jumping out into traffic. Should a dog attempt to get out before you've told him it's his turn, tell him "ah-ah" to give him a chance to think it over. If he sits back down to wait, praise him and then, when you're ready, give him the all clear to jump down. If he jumps down before he should, put or ask him to get back in. Close the vehicle door. Get the rest of the dogs out, or if he's the only or last one, wait 30 seconds or so. Open the door to try again. This procedure is essentially the same one you use to control jumping when you pick a dog up.

Now you're on your walk. If it's a leash walk, insist that dogs maintain slack in the lead at all times. In other words, no pulling. You can do that through training or the use of humane anti-pull equipment.

Chapter 7 covers the training. We'll talk about equipment later in this chapter.

If you and the dogs are lucky enough to have a place to play off leash, don't take that leash off for free. Ask each dog to sit. If you're carrying treats you might give each dog a sample to let them know what awaits them for a good recall. Then, while they are sitting calmly, remove their leashes and tell them, "Go play!" If a dog sits and then pops back up to a stand, ask for another sit and wait until he has held it for several seconds before you unclip the leash. This is another exercise in tone setting and impulse control.

Give lots of feedback

Once the dogs are off leash it shouldn't be a free-for-all. You want to maintain the tone you worked so hard to set, and you want to keep the dogs safe. Practice lots of recalls, reinforcing the dogs each time, and reward all voluntary check-ins by giving dogs a treat each time they come near you. Behavior that's rewarded increases in frequency, so rewarding dogs for coming near you means they'll choose to stick closer by. For dogs on leash, reward voluntary watches. Give the dogs a treat anytime they look back at you or make eye contact. Over a short time, this will give you dogs who choose to keep focused on you during their walk. Such dogs are more likely to hear and respond to your cues, and less likely to be the dogs out at the end of the leash barely aware you're there.

You can use life rewards, too. If you walk a fetch-obsessed dog, reward a good recall by throwing a ball or stick or pine cone. Have swimmers? Ask for a recall or sit before letting your pack charge into the pond. Use life rewards for dogs walking on leash, too. Reward a sit or watch with access to a tree or pole a dog is straining to sniff. Ask for a sit before allowing a dog to say hello to a person on the street. You can use anything a dog wants—a chance to play with another dog, access to a tree that needs marking, even your attention—as a reward for practicing a cue you want to build into or maintain as a reliable behavior.

Time-out inappropriate play behavior

Monitoring play is a big part of the job when walking groups. It's important to give dogs lots of feedback while they're playing. Cheer them on when they're interacting appropriately: "Good job, guys! Nice work! Yay!" But also let them know when you don't approve. If you have any of the difficult play styles you'll see described later in this chapter—Tarzans and bullies in particular—or you have a dog who humps excessively and is getting himself into trouble with other dogs, you want to be ready to intervene. Your goal is to be proactive about avoiding scuffles or fights and helping the dog become a better player.

Step 1. Identify the unwanted behavior. Decide what's okay and what isn't for a particular dog. Then think about how the unwanted behavior usually begins. You don't want to wait to give feedback until a dog has already been humping another dog for 30 seconds; that's not proactive. What does the beginning of the humping sequence look like? What precedes it? Perhaps you've noticed that after a few moments, play starts to heat up and then the dog in question—we'll call him Spot—starts to maneuver toward the back of the other dog. You want to interrupt about then—as play is getting ramped up. The goal is to short-circuit the sequence that leads to trouble.

Step 2. Praise Spot for getting it right. While play is going well, praise Spot—let him know he's doing well.

Step 3. Give a warning cue. As soon as you see the tell-tail sign that the unwanted unwanted sequence is beginning, give your warning cue. This could be "ah-ah" or "easy" or "careful" or "shazam." Dogs don't speak English, so what you say doesn't matter. Just choose something and use it consistently.

If Spot responds to the warning, praise him cheerfully. "Good boy! Nice play!"

Step 4. Give the time-out. If Spot does not heed your warning and instead continues the sequence and makes a move to go to the back of the dog to hump, tell him, "Too bad!" and execute a time-out by looping a leash around his neck and removing him from play.

"Too bad" (or whatever you choose to say) is the time-out cue. It helps Spot learn what's earning him time-outs. In training terms, we're marking an unwanted behavior. Saying something silly like "too bad" or "oh well" also reminds us to stay calm; no need to get worked up. Spot isn't trying to be naughty. He just doesn't understand how to play properly and you're helping him learn.

The time-out itself is a consequence. This is another example of learning by consequence, or operant conditioning. What we're telling Spot is, "When you play that way, play will end." The time-out should be short—30 to 60 seconds—and then Spot should be released to try again. If you're using the time-out procedure consistently (which is critical to its success) and not seeing change over a couple of weeks, you might up the ante by giving a longer time-out on the very first incident each day; perhaps even ending play altogether for that day and keeping Spot on leash.

Time-outs can be used during on-leash walks. When dogs are running free, being put on leash is a bummer of a consequence. But what if they're already on leash? Follow the same time-out procedure and then, for the time-out itself, try making the leash quite short, so that Spot can only walk right next to you instead of sniffing about. Or you can even simply stop and stand stock still in one place on a shortened leash for 30 seconds. Don't talk or look at Spot during this time or interact with him in any other way. In other words, the time-out is 30 seconds of boredom.

When the time-out procedure is followed consistently, you'll see Spot begin to self-regulate. He'll begin to anticipate your warning cue and automatically take the play down a notch, or take a quick break (this could be in the form of shaking off, pausing, a head turn away from his playmate, etc.) before you give the cue. Praise like crazy when this happens. And pat yourself on the back, too!

Equipment to help manage pulling

You can get nice leash walking in two ways: you can train it, or you can manage it. Training for nice leash walking is an involved process. We cover it in Chapter 7. If you'd like to save yourself the time, particularly if you're walking large, strong dogs with a history of pulling or if you're already walking a group of dogs and don't have the luxury of training each separately, you might opt for managing the pulling by using anti-pull equipment. Understand that dogs will not learn not to pull; as soon as you remove the equipment they'll go right back to their pulling ways. But while it's on, you'll be saved a trip to the chiropractor. And since you're being paid to walk your client's dog, not to train him, you should feel no guilt about choosing this option.

There are many humane anti-pulling equipment choices these days. Avoid choke chains and prong collars. They are only minimally effective and we now know from studies that they do, without a doubt, cause tracheal damage over a dog's lifetime.

Humane choices fall into two categories: head halters and anti-pull harnesses. There are many styles and brands of each. Experiment to find the ones you like best.

Head halters

Head halters fit around the dog's upper snout and the back of his head behind the ears. These are the most effective in controlling pulling. As the dog pulls, his head is turned down and so he stops—he can't see where he's going. They also give you the most control, as you can actually use the leash to turn the dog's head, and thus his body, back toward you. The downside to head halters is that most dogs have to be desensitized to wearing them; they have learn to get used to them and this can be a bit of a process. The process is worth it, though, for very large, strong dogs and for any dogs with leash reactivity—dogs who bark and lunge when they see other dogs, people, moving objects, etc. In these cases, it's helpful to be able to gently turn the dog's head away from the objects he's reactive to. The Gentle Leader® is the most well-known head halter, followed by the Halti®. The Halti is an excellent choice for brachycephalic dogs— those with short snouts. There are plenty of other great choices as well.

Anti-pull harnesses

Anti-pull harnesses are a great choice for small to medium dogs or larger dogs who are only moderate pullers. These harnesses (not to be confused with regular harnesses, which actually allow dogs to pull harder!) apply gentle pressure against the upper front legs when dogs pull. Hard to walk when this happens, so dogs back off. The SENSE-ation®, SENSE-ible®, and Easy Walk™ harnesses are three of the most well-known, but, again, there are many choices to consider.

Managing dog-dog types

Now that you've set the tone for your walk, let's talk about recognizing and managing the various dog-dog interaction styles and issues. Much of this section deals specifically with dogs walked in groups, but there are tips sprinkled throughout for walkers taking just one dog at a time.

Avoid taking more than one of these project dogs into a group at a time. A project dog will demand a disproportionate amount of your attention and energy. Two project dogs will make it difficult to address the needs of each dog and of the rest of your pack as well, and to keep everyone safe.

Asocial/proximity-sensitive dogs

These dogs don't enjoy the company of other dogs. In fact, they would prefer other dogs weren't around, or at least that they keep their distance and leave them alone. Asocial/proximity-sensitive (A/PS) dogs often raise their lips, snarl, growl, or even snap at dogs who venture too close. They may have one or two hard-won dog friends, but it generally takes a long time to form new dog relationships and they are very selective about who they hang out with. Development of this personality type generally happens in early adulthood, between one and three years of age. Lack of early socialization is a major factor, and the behavior is fear- or anxiety-based.

Walking an asocial/proximity-sensitive dog on leash

- This dog will be happier on his own, but it's possible to walk him with a small group of carefully chosen pack mates. They should be older, calmer dogs who read body language well and respect the dog's wish to be ignored.

- When walking in a group, unload all the other dogs first. Don't unload this dog until you're ready to go, so you can leash him up and immediately get moving, helping to take other dogs' attention off him.

- Actively scan the environment for other dogs.

- Avoid passing other dogs closely if possible.

- When passing another dog is a necessity, keep the A/PS dog focused on you with a food lure, a "Let's Go," by playing the "Find It" game (see Chapter 7 for instructions on teaching these games), or with happy talk. Move by the other dog quickly. (Do not use "Find It" if the other dog is off leash or if you are walking a group, to avoid resource fights.)

- Reserving a special treat the A/PS dog gets only when he's passing another dog can help over time to lessen his anxiety during these moments. (Be sure he gets these treats as the other dog is approaching and passing; waiting until after the pass is complete won't have the same impact.)

Walking an asocial/proximity-sensitive dog off leash

- The A/PS dog is more comfortable off leash, as that allows him to create social distance for himself. If off leash, allow the dog to avoid other dogs if he chooses to do so.

- Actively scan the environment for other dogs.

- Avoid passing unknown dogs closely if possible.

- If passing another dog is a necessity, keep the A/PS dog focused on you with a food lure, a "Let's Go," or with happy talk. Move by the other dog quickly.

- If walking groups, choose pack mates carefully—they should be older, calmer dogs who read body language well and respect the dog's wish to be left alone.

- Reserving a special treat the A/PS dog gets only when he's passing another dog or when pack mates approach can help over time to lessen his anxiety during these moments.

Tarzans

Tarzan dogs love to play with other dogs, but their social skills are a bit lacking. Think of them as the kid on the playground who puts other kids off by trying too hard and failing to read the other children's signals. Tarzans get themselves in trouble by coming on too strong; they engage in what trainers sometimes call "gross greetings." These dogs run up to other dogs fast and straight on, usually face-to-face rather than any back-end sniffing. They will sometimes get overwhelmed and nip during the greeting, or be reprimanded by the other dog for their impertinence and rude behavior. When they're able to get past the greeting to play, their play tends to be exaggerated—huge, floppy, excited movements. Tarzans are usually young males, most commonly between the ages of 10 months and a year. Their behavior may be due to poor socialization coupled with a great excitement about other dogs. They often don't get enough chances to play with dogs and so are overly motivated when they do.

Walking a Tarzan on leash

- You will likely not be able to walk a Tarzan on leash with a group, as he will be too focused on playing with the other dogs.

- We don't recommend allowing him to greet other dogs on leash until the behavior has been brought under control, as it's likely to lead to snarking incidents. Instead, keep him focused on you if passing another dog is necessary, and pass quickly. Give him a special treat for passing nicely, as he's likely to be disappointed at not getting to say hi. Teaching him to expect a treat for passing other dogs lowers the likelihood of him developing barrier frustration and beginning to lunge and whine or bark at the sight of another dog he can't get close to.

Walking a Tarzan off leash

- Integrate him with well-socialized and tolerant older dogs who will give him appropriate feedback but who aren't likely to take enough offense to start a fight.

- Have him say hello to his pack mates while still on leash so you can help control the speed and tone of the greeting; if he comes on too strong or nips or growls during the greeting, time him out by moving him away from the other dogs. Give him a moment to compose himself and then let him try again. When he gets the greeting right, allow him some off-leash playtime.

- Reinforce polite interactions with verbal praise and by allowing him to continue playing—that's his top-of-the-hierarchy life reward.

- Use time-outs for over-the-top play behavior and for inappropriate greetings of new dogs (avoid non-pack dogs whenever possible, as always).

- Build a strong recall so you can call your Tarzan out of play periodically for a quick focus break before sending him back to continue his game. This keeps things from getting too heated and over time teaches him to take short breaks on his own, thus reducing the likelihood that play becomes too excited and tips over into a squabble.

Bullies

Bullies are just what they sound like. Imagine the school-yard bully from your childhood; most likely he targeted younger and/or shy or fearful kids. Canine bullies do the same thing, and they find it very reinforcing. They will target a younger or fearful dog for play and pester him despite all body language signals that the other dog doesn't want to play. They may follow the shy dog around at close proximity, or bark in his face, or put their paws on his body. These dogs do have play skills and will engage in play with dogs who are willing, but their play often gets stuck in a rut. For example, they may do all the chasing and not allow themselves to be chased. Or insist on always being on top in a wrestling game, instead of taking their turn on the bottom. And they are unlikely to heed body language cues from another dog who no longer wishes to be chased or wrestled with.

Walking a bully on leash

- If you're walking a bully on leash in a group, walk him with older, confident dogs.
- Avoid on-leash greetings of unknown dogs.

Walking a bully off leash

- Integrate him with well-socialized and tolerant older dogs who will give him appropriate feedback, but aren't likely to take enough offense to start a fight.
- Reinforce polite interactions and appropriate play with verbal praise and by allowing the bully to continue playing.
- Use time-outs for over-the-top play behavior and for inappropriate greetings of new dogs (avoid non-pack dogs whenever possible, as always).
- Build a strong recall so you can call him out of play periodically for a quick focus break before sending him back to continue his game. This keeps things from getting too heated and over time teaches the dog to take short breaks on his own, thus reducing the likelihood that the play becomes stuck in a rut and tips over into a squabble.

Resource guarders

These dogs are fine with other dogs except in the presence of a coveted resource. When a coveted resource is present, they may growl and snap to keep other dogs away from it, and even fight if they feel their resource is threatened. Most commonly dogs guard food or favorite objects. Food can include the treats you carry, but also things we humans might not consider edible, such as a dead fish on the beach or a decomposing deer leg on a trail, or even a fresh deposit of horse or cow manure. Objects worthy of guarding may include things like tennis balls, a good stick, or even a pine cone you've tossed for the dogs to play with. Dogs may also guard space, such as the interior of your vehicle or the few feet or even yards of real estate around themselves anywhere they happen to sit or lie down for more than a few minutes. Keep these dogs moving. Finally, some dogs will guard you. You are, after all, the source of all things good—food, attention, the walk that is the highlight of their day. They may growl or snap at other dogs who attempt to approach you.

Walking resource guarders on leash

- This should provide no great challenge; just be sure not to offer the dog a treat or toy in the presence of another dog if that is his trigger. Or teach the dogs to reach only for their own treats by playing the name-the-treat game so there are no squabbles. (Name-the-treat is easy to teach: simply say each dog's name before you hand him a treat, every time. Soon the dogs will realize there's no point reaching for a treat when they haven't heard their own name first.)

Walking resource guarders off leash

- Again, all should be well as long as resources are kept under control. For example, if you have a ball guarder, don't throw the ball in the presence of other dogs. If you're walking a group, leave balls at home.

- If you have a dog who guards objects you can't control, such as sticks, be sure to walk him in a group of dogs who don't care about sticks and will read his body language and leave him alone when he has one. And it's best to not walk more than one resource guarder in a group.

- If you have a dog who guards your bait bag or you, give him a treat whenever another dog comes near. This teaches him that having other dogs around is not so bad. Never treat him when other dogs aren't present. If he snarks at other dogs, give the dog who was snarked at the treat instead, helping the guarder to learn that snarking doesn't pay.

Barrier-frustrated or leash-reactive dogs

There are two types of leash reactivity. Some dogs react to other dogs with barking, lunging, growling, etc., when on leash. This is pure frustration. They want so badly to interact with other dogs that, over time, their growing frustration at never getting to say hello turns into this big, noisy display. This is called hyper-motivated reactivity. Other dogs bark, lunge, and growl out of fear. Fear-based reactive displays are a dog's attempt to manipulate social distance. They're on leash and thus can't move themselves away from the other dog, so instead they growl and lunge, hoping to convince the other dog to move away. In most cases, both types of dogs are fine with other dogs when they themselves are off leash.

Walking leash-reactive dogs

- Practice vigilant situational awareness and avoid other dogs whenever possible. Keep as much distance from other dogs as possible when you can't completely avoid them.

- Begin using happy talk as soon as your dog sees the other dog, then distract your dog with a food lure or a game of "Find It." The trick is to keep your dog from looking at the other dog.

- Move quickly past other dogs, but keep calm.

- For dogs who can't yet be distracted, use visual barriers such as stepping behind a parked car or blocking the dog's view with your body. A head halter can also help, as it allows you to control the direction of the dog's head, and thus turn him away from the other dog.

- Treat this dog only when other dogs are present, or reserve the best treats for these occasions. Doing so will, over time, help the dog realize that the presence of other dogs is actually a good thing, rather than a cause for frustration or alarm.

"Police" dogs

Think of these dogs as the fun police. They tend to charge in whenever other dogs are playing to shut down the activity. They are usually adult females who have lost their interest in reindeer games and would prefer a quiet, calm atmosphere without all these youngsters galloping about.

Walking police dogs on leash

- Walking these girls on leash should provide no problems, even in a group. In fact, they may be helpful if you're having difficulty keeping younger dogs moving forward instead of trying to play with each other.

Walking police dogs off leash

- If walking in a group, it's generally better to walk them with other adult dogs who aren't interested in playing either, to avoid putting a damper on the fun of younger dogs.

- When other dogs do play, reinforce the police dog for leaving them alone. You might even distract her with a game of her own, like fetch, or with treats. Treating her whenever other dogs play will help her relax about this activity over time.

- Time her out for any policing by putting her on leash.

Inter-male aggression

This most commonly happens when intact males are present. What's often not understood, however, is that it's usually the altered male who starts the conflict. Unneutered males are more threatening to all other males and their scent can trigger aggression in other males—intact or not. Essentially, intact males have a bull's-eye on them. Sometimes intact males will become proactive aggressors themselves, having become sensitized to the presence of male dogs from repeated attacks.

Walking intact males on leash

- This is the safest course for intact males. You can keep them close and intervene before trouble erupts.

- If you're walking intact males on leash in a group, choose primarily females as walking companions. Carefully introduce any male candidates to make sure they aren't interested in targeting the intact male (not all will).

Walking altered males who attack intact males on leash

- Watch the environment and take a wide berth around other males if you see that they are intact or are unable to determine whether they are.

- Keep the dog focused on you with a "Watch," "Leave It," or "Find It" as you pass intact males, avoiding greetings.

Walking intact males off leash

It is safe to walk intact males off leash only in the following circumstances:

- Walking in wide-open spaces in which you can see other dogs coming from far off. Whenever another dog is approaching, leash the intact dog immediately as a safety precaution. You are less likely to have him attacked while he's on leash, and you cannot protect him if a greeting takes place away from you. Keep him focused on you while passing other dogs and avoid greetings.

- The intact dog you are walking has a very strong recall. Build a strong recall to make sure you can call this dog to you for leashing up when you see other dogs approaching. Also be sure to call him immediately when you see him air sniff (sniff the air with his head tipped back). The other risk involved in walking intact males is their tendency to wander when they catch the scent of a female in heat.

Walking altered males who attack other males off leash

It is safe to walk males who attack other males off leash only in the following circumstances:

- Walking in wide-open spaces in which you can see other dogs coming from far off. Whenever another dog is approaching, leash the dog immediately as a safety precaution. Keep him focused on you while passing male dogs and avoid greetings.

- The dog you are walking has a very strong recall. Build a strong recall to make sure you can call this dog to you for leashing up when you see other dogs approaching. Also be sure to call him immediately when you see him air sniff (sniff the air with his head tipped back) in case he is catching the scent of another male dog. You want to catch him before he heads off to investigate. If you cannot call a dog with this issue reliably, he should not be allowed off leash.

High prey drive-related behavior

Many breeds are given to prey behavior toward other dogs. Border Collies are a prime example—they are likely to crouch down when seeing another dog and then slowly stalk toward the dog, finally springing forward in greeting. Though there's usually nothing ominous intended by this behavior, it can be off-putting or anxiety-inducing for other dogs, upsetting to dog owners, and can even cause conflict when the dog being greeted takes offense. Another form high prey drive can take is unwelcomed chasing, in which the dog chases another dog in an intense way not seen as consensual play by the chasee. Some dogs will redirect their prey drive onto other moving objects—lunging at passing bicycles, joggers, skateboards, even cars.

Walking high prey drive dogs on leash

- Coax dogs out of any crouching behavior and ask them to walk alongside you. Use treats or cues ("Watch" or "Find it," for example) to help them focus on you instead of the other dog as you pass by quickly. The most difficult moment will be right as the other dog (or person or thing) passes, particularly if it is moving briskly. Ask for a "Watch" or "Find It" as the dog, person, or object approaches, and reward your dog for removing his focus from whatever is passing. If he is too excited to respond to the cue, get out a treat and time things so you're delivering a treat at that moment. Over time, the dog will begin to look at you for his treat as things pass by. At that point, you can begin asking for a "Watch" or "Find It."

- Always keep the leash short during passings to make sure your dog is unable to lunge at the passing dog, person, or wheels.

- It's best not to walk dogs who lunge at other dogs in an on-leash group, as their behavior will often engage others in the group to participate. The dog given to lunging may also redirect the lunge onto group mates in his frustration at not being able to reach whatever or whomever is passing.

Walking high prey drive dogs off leash

It's safe to walk dogs with high prey drive off leash only in the following circumstances:

- Walking in wide-open spaces in which you can see other dogs, people, bicycles, etc. coming from far off. Whenever another dog, jogger, or moving object is approaching, leash the high prey drive dog immediately as a safety precaution. Keep him focused on you while passing.

- The dog you are walking has a very strong recall. Build a strong recall to make sure you can call this dog to you for leashing up when you see his triggers approaching.

- You select pack mates carefully. Follow the 50% rule to protect against predatory drift, as discussed in Chapter 4. Choose dogs who don't react with fear or snarking to the high prey drive dog's stalking behavior.

Handling other trail, beach, park, and sidewalk users

Walking dogs would be relatively easy if it were just the dogs. But you share the spaces you walk in with many others—other dog walkers, people walking their own dogs, people who want to say hello to your dogs, people who are afraid of your dogs. Some of you also share trail space with horseback riders and even the occasional field of cows or sheep or goats. Having a clear plan for sharing your walking spaces with other users will make encountering them much easier and less stressful.

In all interactions with others, recognize your role as an ambassador. You represent not only your own business (or the business you work for), but also dog walking as a profession and dogs in general. You may not wish this, but it's true. Every interaction people have with you influences how they perceive and feel about your business, about dog walkers, about dogs. The guiding principle in every interaction is to attempt to leave the person thinking to herself, "Wow, what a great dog walker. Those dogs were so well behaved." Because when it comes time to vote or weigh in on leash laws, on dog parks, on access for dogs to local trailheads, etc., you want the people you've encountered to be more pro-dog for the experience.

They can't bite if they can't reach

In general, do your best to keep the dogs in your care from interacting with other dogs and people, even if the dogs you walk are easygoing and friendly. The only surefire way to avoid an incident is to avoid contact. Though there will be plenty of people and dogs who would like to say hello, your job is to keep the dogs you walk safe, and there's no better way to do that than limiting contact with dogs and people you don't know and whose behavior you can't predict.

There are two primary ways to limit contact when passing other dogs and people—one is to move by quickly with your dogs' attention on you using a "Watch" cue and your voice to keep them attentive, and the other is to pull to the side, gather your dogs' attention with a "Sit/Stay" (see Chapter 7 for how to train this), and let others pass.

It's generally better to pass other dogs, regardless of whether you're walking on leash on a busy sidewalk or on or off leash on a trail, beach, etc. Pulling over to allow passing dogs often backfires, as the passing dogs may stop to investigate your crew. Better to get your dogs' eyes on you and pass briskly. The faster you move and the more you chatter, the more interesting and distracting you make yourself. Using a food lure can help immensely as well. Be sure to reward good, attentive passing behavior—you'll get more of it that way.

In most cases it's preferable to pull over to let people pass. This is especially true if you're walking a group of dogs, whether off leash in an open or trail setting or on leash on a narrow sidewalk. Don't make others work to get around you. And it can be intimidating to see a group of dogs approach, even if you're a dog lover. Better that you pull your dogs over, ask them to sit, and keep them focused on you. This is an impressive sight to other trail or sidewalk users, and a wonderful display of professional courtesy. Whenever possible or appropriate, acknowledge the passersby with a hello.

If you notice a person seeming nervous or anxious about passing you, acknowledge him before he fully approaches. Give him a friendly, "I've got them nice and focused if you want to go ahead and pass." If your dogs are off leash, tell him, "I'll go ahead and leash them up for you," and then do so, even if you know your dogs have a solid "Sit/Stay" and don't require the leashing. In short, do everything you can to make sure the people who encounter you and your dogs have a better day for it.

If you're walking a single dog or a small group on a busy sidewalk, you aren't likely to make much progress by stopping for each person you need to pass. In those situations, keep up a brisk pace with the dogs walking close to you. Ask dogs who show an interest in passersby to "Watch" you each time someone passes, giving them a food reward each time. You'll soon have them trained to look at you instead of your fellow sidewalk users. (Once this behavior is consistent, you can begin reducing the rewards so you treat the dogs occasionally for looking at you, rewarding with verbal praise in between. Watch the dogs' behavior carefully so you can find the right rate of reinforcement to keep them paying attention to you consistently.)

Although occasional interactions with others cannot always be helped, strive to keep them at a minimum. Avoid all contact between dogs and children, even if you believe the dogs to be comfortable with kids. The only way to be sure nothing happens is to not allow the opportunity, and the stakes of a mistake here are just too high. Also, protect shy dogs at all times. Some people, believing themselves to be "dog people," will want to force interactions with dogs who aren't comfortable with strangers. While it can be uncomfortable to prevent someone from petting a dog, your job is protect the dogs in your care. Find a nice way to say no, but do say no. ("She's quite shy and isn't ready to make new friends yet." Or "Our policy is not to allow the dogs to say hello. They're all friendly, but we have a strict no-risk policy. I'm sorry about that.")

Practicing good pack management keeps the dogs in your care safe, reduces your liability risks, and makes sure that everyone has a great day—you, your dogs, and everyone you encounter. It's also great for business. Who wouldn't entrust their dog to the walker whose dogs are so beautifully behaved?

Chapter 6

Driving Dogs: Car Manners
and Safety

If the walking service you provide requires you to transport dogs, particularly in groups, this chapter will help you with what can be one of the most complex aspects of dog walking. That may surprise you, but consider the implications of multiple dogs packed into a tight space for an extended period of time. Much the same as with humans, getting along can be harder when you can't get away.

Many a group walker has said of a skirmish breaking out early on the walk, "I don't know what happened. There didn't seem to be any reason for the fight." There's always a reason, and in these cases it may well have occurred on the drive to the park. Tensions escalate in the vehicle and walkers drive along unawares, keeping eyes on the road and thus missing all the subtle (and perhaps some fairly overt) body language going on behind. When the dogs are finally freed, it takes only a small spark to flare already fanned tempers.

Fights shortly after a trip, and those that more alarmingly take place in the car during the trip, likely have to do with one of these triggers:

- Dogs bumping into each other, such as when the vehicle takes a corner.

- Space guarding, in which one dog attempts to keep others out of his space—a difficult task in an enclosed and moving vehicle.

- Dogs not able to move away from each other. Remember from Chapter 4 that most dogs in conflict will choose flight over a fight. Fights are much more common when that choice is removed.

- Barrier frustration caused by attempts to separate dogs. Separation by use of crates, gates, tethers, or seat belts can keep dogs from fighting or being injured while the car takes a corner or in a crash, but if dogs are able to see each other, you can get the same type of results you see with leash-reactive dogs or dogs who fence-fight. The frustration at not being able to interact properly can build to the point of conflict once the dogs are out of the car and able to reach each other. In short, it's never wise to set up a situation where dogs can engage in long bouts of staring.

What to do? Vehicle choice matters a lot, as does vehicle set up. Ideally you want a vehicle that's large enough to accommodate the number of dogs you transport, with all dogs crated separately. Vans are the most flexible and useful in this regard, though SUVs and even wagons may work for smaller and medium dogs. (If you use a cargo van rather than a passenger van, make sure there's an adequate airflow system in the back.) If you can't fit enough crates in your vehicle, or you have dogs who don't crate well, use vehicle gates to separate dogs into smaller groupings, and choose who rides with whom carefully.

Beware the pickups

You may be tempted to go for a pickup truck with a shell on the back, but although trucks have their advantages (the noise and mess being contained in the back large among them), they are the least safe option for the dogs. You can't see or hear what's going on back there, so there's no chance of stepping in early to defuse conflict. And conflict is much more likely in a truck, where dogs are loose together, bumping into each other, and unable to move away from each other.

Pickup trucks are also dangerous because of the large amount of real estate you must keep dogs from escaping from. The back of a pickup truck is much wider than the space of an opened car or van door, and it's all too easy for a dog to jump down before you're ready or while you're loading another dog.

To the extent you can, set your crates and gates up so dogs don't see each other. You can use lightweight opaque barriers between crates, for example. Another advantage of this is that dogs who can't see out the windows can't bark at passing dogs, people, bicycles, etc., making your trip easier and safer.

Which crates?

There are three main styles of crates: hard plastic (Vari-Kennel® is the most common), wire cage, and soft mesh. The first two are excellent choices for stacking, such as in a van or tall SUV. (Be sure to carefully secure stacked crates.) Wire crates and mesh crates are best for airflow, while plastic crates are best for keeping barrier frustration at a minimum. You'll likely want to use either wire or mesh crates if your walking vehicle is also your everyday ride, as they both collapse quickly and easily. Mesh crates are particularly good for dual-purpose vehicles as they keep dog hair, mud, and more unmentionable messes contained. Should a dog soil a mesh crate, simply hose the crate out, spray it with disinfectant, and hose it again. Wire crates are easily cleaned, but there's a high chance that whatever it was that needed cleaning will also end up on your upholstery. Plastic crates also clean easily, but they don't collapse without the tedious removal of multiple screws.

You can also give crated or otherwise individually separated dogs stuffed Kongs® or other chewables to keep them occupied during the drive. This is especially helpful for dogs who bark or whine their way to the trailhead—it's difficult to keep up the barking when you're busy licking peanut butter from a red rubber cone. Another good trick is to toss treats into the back of crates to motivate car-wary dogs to hop in, and as a reward for all dogs at the end of a walk. This is a great practice for off-leash walkers, as a high-value treat in the truck can help guard against dogs who go wandering at the end of a walk in order to draw out the fun. (For them, that is—not so fun for the walker.)

Never allow a dog to be loose in your car such that he is able to jump into your lap or into the footwell; this can and does cause car accidents. Also note that airbags can easily kill dogs, just as they do children. If you have a dog riding up front with you, he should be in a firm crate (preferably plastic Vari-Kennel style). If he can't be crated, use a canine seatbelt and disarm your airbag.

Should a fight break out while you're driving despite all your careful planning, or should a dog need care or attention for any reason, wait until you can safely pull over. As you'll recall from Chapter 4, the chances of the dogs doing serious damage to each other is much smaller than the chances of you and the dogs being harmed in a car accident.

Loading and unloading

In Chapter 5 we talked about setting the tone at the beginning of the walk, how doing so starts before the walk gets underway, in fact, by insisting on a polite greeting at the client's door and a controlled walk to your vehicle. Tone setting continues at the car.

Dogs should be asked to hold a sit before being invited up into the vehicle. If the dog will be joining other dogs in a shared space in your car, those dogs should be asked to sit as well. This is partly to keep them from jumping out while the new dog is jumping in, and partly to keep them from greeting the newcomer too intrusively. Treat the dogs for allowing their pack mate to join them, and treat the dog who has just jumped in as well. This will help the dogs build a positive association with riding together.

At the parking lot or trailhead, each dog should sit before being invited with a release word to jump down from the vehicle. Say "sit" once and wait for it. Use a hand signal or food lure if needed in the beginning, as dogs will be very excited to get their walk underway, and focusing on your requests will be challenging. If a dog begins to exit the car before you've given him the release word (use a clear word, such as "okay" or "jump"), tell him "ah-ah." If he backs up, ask him to sit and try again. If he jumps down, put him back in the car, close the door, and let someone else out before you try the first dog again. Just like the jumping at the front door, the message is clear: "If you want to get down, you have to sit and wait. Jumping down before I say okay won't work." And just like all training, consistency is key here—don't ever rush this process, no matter how late you're running; you'll only cause considerably more work for yourself tomorrow and the days after.

This process is made easier by carefully choosing the order in which you let the dogs out. (And this is another advantage of crates—they help control the environment so you can get one dog out at a time, keeping things calm and avoiding any tragic mishaps, such as a dog jumping down and running into traffic.) Think about the dogs in your group. Get the calmer, more focused dogs out of the car first. These will be easier to handle while you're getting your more rambunctious charges out.

When reloading at the end of the walk, toss high-value treats into the back of each dog's crate to help with speedy loading and to create a positive end of walk ritual.

Chapter 7

Building Basic Obedience

Why would you learn obedience training as a dog walker?

Simply, to make the job easier. For an easier time getting past distractions like squirrels, children, garbage on the ground, and other dogs. For an easier time getting and keeping a dog's attention. For an easier time keeping off-leash charges nearby, and the peace of mind of knowing they will come when you call. Walking dogs is fun. Walking calm, responsive dogs is a blast. It's also good marketing; nothing looks quite as impressive as a dog walker in full charge of her cheerful four-legged clients.

Dog walkers don't learn training to change dogs' behavior for their owners. That's a trainer's job. In fact, giving training advice if you aren't a trainer is both unethical and dangerous. Your liability coverage as a dog walker likely won't cover you for trouble arising from sharing training advice. If your clients need training assistance, refer them to a training colleague; it's safer and it's good networking for your business, too.

The five key training concepts you need to make your job easier:

1. Reinforce behavior you like—you'll get more of it

Remember, dogs do what works. We're very quick to tell children, dogs, and those below us at work "no." We're always quick to punish. But we'd get more done by saying "yes" more often, and rewarding good behavior. Remember operant conditioning from Chapter 2: rewarded behavior increases and ignored behavior decreases. Is a dog sitting nicely? Find a way to tell him thanks. When an off-leash dog checks in with you, let him know you appreciate it with a treat or the throw of a ball. Like it when a dog comes when you call? Don't make the mistake of not reinforcing that behavior.

2. Use life rewards

Giving a treat is an effective way to tell a dog what you like. But it's not the only way. As a dog walker, you hold control over many items on a dog's list of favorite things: having a leash clipped on for a walk, having the door opened to the wonderful outdoors, having a leash taken off for some free play, having a ball thrown, being allowed to move forward on leash toward a good smell or item to investigate, and so forth.

You can use these life rewards to build a wonderfully mannered dog simply by asking for polite behavior to gain access to them. If a dog wants her leash clipped on, she'll need to sit for it. Would she like her ball thrown? Another sit. Want to go smell the hydrant? No problem, so long as there's no pulling to get there. Using life rewards creates a systematic way to train the dogs in your care as you go about your time with them.

3. Don't reinforce behavior you don't like

It's a simple concept, but so easy to forget in practice. A dog barks and we forget ourselves and throw the ball. A dog jumps on us when we enter his home and we leash him up for the walk anyway. We allow dogs to pull us down the sidewalk. But dogs do what works, and unless you like to be barked at, jumped on, or dragged along, be careful not to reinforce these and any other behaviors you don't want to see more of.

4. Remove rewards for behavior you don't like

Unfortunately, just ignoring behavior you don't like won't always be enough to make it go away. To have a quicker impact on behavior, remove the reward the dog is after. Instead of throwing the ball for a dog who is barking at you to do so, walk away from it. (Or, even better, pick it up and put it in your pocket for a minute or two.) When a dog jumps on you as you enter his house, turn around and leave. Stand on the front porch for a moment before trying again. Repeat this as many times as needed. When the dog finally does not jump on you, reward him by clipping on his leash. (You may need to plan some extra time for the first few days of this training, but it's well worth the effort if you don't like being jumped on.)

5. Be consistent

Behavioral science has repeatedly shown a disturbing fact: intermittent reinforcement strengthens behavior. That's why dogs who are only occasionally fed at the table become such dedicated beggars. (It's also why gambling is so addictive.) So be careful; once you decide to no longer reinforce behaviors like pulling, barking, or jumping, stick to your guns. You can work consistently for weeks on teaching a dog not to pull on leash, but it only takes bending the rules one day when you're feeling rushed to undo all that work.

Do I have to use food?

No, but your job will be easier if you do. Reinforced behavior increases in frequency, and food is the easiest, quickest, and most effective reinforcer for most dogs. It's easy to carry, quick to deliver, and at the top of most dogs' hierarchies of good things.

Now, I know what at least some readers will be thinking at this point: isn't that a bribe? Honestly, I've never really understood this question. Giving a dog a piece of food for doing something you asked of him is no more a bribe than giving a child a reward for a good grade, nice manners, or a clean room. Why is it acceptable to tell a child to eat her vegetables in order to get her dessert, but we can't stomach the idea of telling a dog to sit for a treat?

Unfortunately I think part of our squeamishness about this comes from a deep-seated belief, sometimes conscious and sometimes not, that dogs should do our bidding simply because we said so. But why should they? Do we really think dogs' purpose on this planet is to serve us out of love and devotion? Why in the world would they do that? They're animals and, like all animals, their purpose is to see to their own needs—food, shelter, reproduction, whatever resource they're interested in at a given point in time. As we talked about in Chapter 2, dogs do what works to get them what they want. And that's okay because we're smarter and we can use that to get what we want.

And just because their sole drive isn't to make us happy doesn't mean they don't deeply enjoy their relationship with us, perhaps even love us if we want to look at it that way. It doesn't in any way diminish the amazing interspecies relationship we have with them.

Sit

Why train "Sit"?

"Sit" is great for building calm, polite behavior. Think of it as a dog's way of saying please. And if you use it a lot, "Sit" can become the dog's default greeting, which stops him from jumping on people.

How to train it

Step 1. *Say it.* Tell the dog, "Sit" in a cheerful tone of voice.

Step 2. *Show it.* Pause a second (one-one thousand), then lure the dog into a sit by putting the treat up to his nose and slowly moving the treat backwards and up. Keep the treat lure close to the dog's nose—if you move your hand up too quickly or too far away from his mouth, he may give up and lose interest.

Step 3. *Pay it.* As soon as the dog's hindquarters hit the ground, praise and treat. Repeat as many times as you can, so long as you and the dog are still enjoying yourselves. Praise and treat every sit.

Step 4. *Repeat it.* Repeat the exercise several times over a few days. When the dog sits reliably, it's time to take the treat out of your hand and use the verbal cue alone. If the dog makes a mistake, first try luring without the treat. Only put the treat back in your hand if all else fails.

Training tip: Only say the cue once. Say it, pause, then lure.

Troubleshooting: If you have trouble with this exercise, try practicing with the dog standing in front of a wall or fence. This way, when you move him back, he has nowhere to go but into a sitting position. Then break the exercise into small steps. First treat the dog for putting his nose in the air. Then wait until he lowers his hindquarters and treat for that. Finally treat generously when the dog's bottom finally touches the ground.

When to practice

Ask for a "Sit" for all life rewards you have to offer the dogs you walk. For example:

- Before throwing a ball, Frisbee, stick, etc.
- Before handing over a treat.
- Before opening a door.

- Before putting on a leash to go for a walk.
- Before taking off a leash at the park or beach.
- Before hopping into or out of the car.

Stay

Why teach "Stay"?
To get individual dogs or a group of dogs to sit and focus on you when distractions move by, for example when stepping to the side of a trail to let a person pass.

How to train "Stay"
Step 1. Stand in front of the dog. Tell the dog, "Stay" in a cheerful tone of voice, pause for a second, then give the "Stay" hand signal: hand out in front of you, palm facing dog. Praise and treat. Repeat a couple of times to get the dog into the game. Tell the dog "Okay" and encourage him to get up.

Step 2. Slowly increase the number of seconds you wait before giving the "Okay" release. Treat the dog every few seconds for maintaining the "Stay."

Step 3. Over time, increase the time between treats. But be sure to mix it up, sometimes treating more frequently.

Handling distractions
Step 1. Keep an eye out for distractions nearby. As soon as a distraction occurs (a dog runs by, for example) praise and treat immediately before the dog breaks his "Stay." The idea is to reward him before he has a chance to make a mistake.

Step 2. If the dog starts to gets up, tell him "ah-ah." If that convinces him hold the "Stay," praise him. Wait a couple of seconds, then reward. If he gets up, tell him "too bad," ask for an easier "Stay," and reward him for that. Then work your way back up.

Training tips:
- Vary the length of the "Stay;" for example, do some that are 20 seconds and some that are 5 seconds.
- When you're working with a group of dogs, practice with each dog individually as he checks in with you. When you're

working them in a group, keep the treats coming, especially when the dogs are learning, and use your voice to keep the dogs focused on you. Treat dogs who are struggling with their "Stays" more often.

Troubleshooting: If the dog gets up, say "too bad" in the same tone of voice you would say "bummer." After a mistake, immediately ask for another "Stay," this one a bit easier, to give the dog a chance to be successful and earn a treat. Then work your way up to the "Stay" that was too difficult.

If the dog is making more than the occasional mistake, you're going too fast. Go back to something easier and work your way up from there. Remember, the secret to teaching "Stay" is to start easy and go slowly.

Wait

Why train "Wait"?
Because door-dashing is a favorite sport of most dogs. It's just so exiting to get to the other side. But in addition to safety issues, "Wait" also helps to establish a calm, focused tone for walks. The "Wait" cue teaches dogs to pause or stop until you give the all clear.

Where to use "Wait"
Use at client's door, to get in and out of your vehicle, to step off curbs to cross the street, etc.

How to teach it
Step 1. At the door, tell the dog "Wait" in a cheerful tone of voice. Reach for the doorknob. If he waits, give him a treat. Repeat several times. Begin to open the door. If he stays in place, give him another treat. Repeat several times. If the dog starts to move to go out, close the door. Without repeating the cue, begin to open the door again. If he stays, treat him. If he starts to move to go out, close the door again. Repeat this action, without repeating the cue, opening the door wider and wider.

Step 2. When the door is open with the dog successfully waiting, give him a cheerful "okay" and let him go out.

Training tips:

- Only give the cue once.

- At first, remember to only open the door a few inches so the dog can't rush out. As the dog gets better, you can then open the door a little more.

- For this method to really take effect you need to be consistent. Ask the dog to "Wait" at every door, every time.

Troubleshooting: If the dog jumps out of your car before you release him, place him back in the vehicle, close the door, and wait a minute or two before giving him another try.

Where else can I use "Wait"?

- All doors (even ones that lead into safe places like your backyard).

- Sidewalk curbs.

- Getting in and out of cars.

Loose-Leash Walking

Why train "Loose-Leash Walking"?

Dogs love to pull to get to whatever is out ahead: great smells, other dogs, open spaces, fun and adventure. Pulling gets dogs to what they want faster. As a strategy, it works. Pulling is rewarding to the dog, so the more he does it, the harder it is for him to give it up. If you don't enjoy being dragged along, you'll have to teach him that pulling no longer works.

How to train "Loose-Leash Walking"

Step 1: The dog learns to stand calmly next to you without pulling away.

1. Load one hand with treats.

2. Praise and treat when the dog is calm and/or looking at you.

3. If the dog pulls away from you, don't yank the leash and don't reel him back in. Stand still and wait until he returns to you. If he is very distracted, call his name.

4. When he comes back to you, praise and treat.

Step 2: The dog learns to stay close to you while walking.

1. With the dog standing calmly next to you, say his name and "let's go."

2. Praise and treat after the first step, as long as he dog doesn't dash forward.

3. Keep walking and praise/treat every other step.

4. Gradually increase the number of steps between rewards.

5. If the dog starts pulling, stop and wait until there's some slack in the leash again. Then take a step with him and reward him quickly for walking near you.

6. Keep him guessing. Sometimes reward after one step, sometimes after five, then again after two, then after seven, and so on.

Training tip: Consistency is key to training nice walking habits, so if you're in a rush, use a humane anti-pull device to protect your training. Anti-pull devices were discussed in Chapter 5.

Troubleshooting: If the dog pulls and you don't get a chance to treat, apply red light/green light. As soon as the dog pulls and the leash goes tight, stop. Wait for the leash to loosen even just a little bit and then walk forward. Be prepared to stop again if the dog pulls again so the leash tightens. The dog needs to learn that a tight leash is a red light that stops the walk. A loose leash is a green light that means more walking.

An alternative to red light/green light is to change direction. When the leash goes tight, turn around and head in the other direction. Over time, this teaches the dog that when he pulls he actually moves farther away from what he's pulling toward.

Let's Go

Why teach "Let's Go"?
Think of "Let's Go" as an on-leash recall. Use it to:

- Get a dog moving again after he has paused to go to the bathroom or check out an interesting smell—without tugging on his leash.

- Recapture his attention from a distraction or to change direction—without having to tug him along.

How to train it
Teach "Let's Go" during your walks, practicing initially at times when the dog isn't greatly distracted.

Step 1. Cheerfully tell the dog "Let's Go!" If he turns toward you, praise him and move in the direction you want to go. Treat him when he catches up. If he doesn't turn toward you, dangle a food treat in front of his nose and lure him in the direction you want to go, treating him once he has followed you a few steps.

Step 2. Repeat the above exercise many times until the dog responds quickly every time. Then begin to practice at times when he is investigating mildly interesting stuff like a smell on the grass, a discarded water bottle, or a noise across the street.

Step 3. When the dog responds despite mild distractions, begin to work on harder ones, such as other dogs, anything edible, or a treed squirrel.

Training tips:
- Only say the cue once.
- The trick to redirecting a dog's attention is to be proactive. Time your "Let's Go!" intervention just as the dog is showing interest in something—don't wait until he is fully engrossed in the distraction.

Hand Target or "Touch"

What is "Touch"?
A cue to get a dog to touch his nose to your hand.

Why teach it?
"Touch" gives you a way to capture a dog's attention and direct his movements. For example, you can ask for a "Touch" to guide a dog past another dog or through a busy urban situation, or to pull his attention away from another dog or other distraction.

How to teach it
Step 1. Present your hand a couple of inches away from the dog's face. Praise and treat for any interest he shows, whether an actual

touch of his nose to your hand or just looking at it. After the first few times, reward only for a full nose touch.

Step 2. Repeat this until the dog reliably touches your hand.

Step 3. Now add the verbal cue. Before presenting your hand, say "Touch" and then put your hand down. (Be sure to pause for a second between the cue and reaching down.)

Step 4. When the dog responds reliably to the verbal cue, begin to increase the distance of the dog's head from your hand by a few inches.

Step 5. Keep increasing the distance little by little.

Step 6. Begin adding movement, walking a bit and praising the dog for staying with you and keeping his nose near your hand.

Training tip: If the dog makes several mistakes in a row, go back a step and make the exercise easier. Even if he's doing great, throw in an easy version every now and again for motivation.

Find It

Why teach it?

"Find It" is an excellent exercise for diverting a dog's attention away from something, such as another dog. It's a particularly useful exercise when walking individual dogs on or off leash, and is used most often for dogs with leash reactivity. ("Find It" is not ideal in group situations, though, as it can easily spark resource guarding fights.)

How to teach it

Step 1. While standing still, say "Find It" in a cheerful tone and toss a treat onto the ground in front of the dog. Repeat many times.

Step 2. Now try it while walking. Say "Find It" and toss the treat in front of the dog, in the direction you're moving. Try to toss the treat such that you and the dog can continue forward momentum. Think of it as bowling with treats.

Step 3. Once the dog has picked up a treat, but before he has turned back to look at you, you can toss another treat. Continue to do this.

This teaches the dog to keep moving forward with his nose to the ground, rather than looking around for other dogs, for example.

Training tips:

- Eventually you can occasionally use "Find It" without tossing a treat, which is helpful in situations where other dogs are close by.

- Choose treats that don't crumble. Small, rounded or square pieces that will roll a bit when you toss them will keep you and the dog moving.

Recall

Why train recall?

So the dog will come when it is truly important.

The 5 rules of recall

1. **Never call the dog for anything unpleasant,** such as nail clipping, bathing, or having his leash clipped on to go home from the park. In short, anything that might give him pause the next time you call him.

2. **Never call the dog if you are not sure he will come.** All recalls should be successful recalls. Work at the dog's level: if he has a kindergarten-level recall, don't give him a graduate assignment like being called away from a cat in a tree.

3. **If you call the dog and he doesn't come, you must make it happen.** Run over to him and put a treat in front of his nose, backing up as you get his attention so he follows you. This is sometimes referred to as "saving the recall."

4. **Never repeat the cue.** Resist the urge to call over and over and over. It only teaches the dog to tune out the cue. Call once and, if necessary, use rule 3. Make the recall happen.

5. **Fabulous rewards get fabulous recalls.** If you want the dog to stop whatever interesting doggie thing he is doing and come running to you, make it worth his while. Use extra yummy treats—no dry biscuits here!—or a well-thrown ball, if that is the dog's fancy.

How to train it

Step 1: Call the dog. Cheerful tones often produce better results—and make sure you are loud enough to be heard, especially in busy environments. Remember to actually give the cue ("Fido, come!"); the dog's name by itself is not a recall.

Step 2: Make yourself interesting. Clap, whistle, squat, throw your arms out, cheer the dog in: "Great, great, faster, you can do it..." When he arrives, spill the treats or throw the ball. If appropriate, release him to go back to whatever he was up to so he doesn't come to view recalls as an end to fun.

Training tips:

- Find an extra yummy treat the dog has never had before but you think he will go crazy for (baby food, Cheez Whiz, liver paste). At the end of the walk when it's time to go home, walk up to him without calling him, leash him up, and give him this extra special treat. Do this consistently and you'll have your dogs lining up to be leashed—instead of running off for an extra 20 minutes of adventure or playing "catch me if you can."

- Practice recall initially in enclosed spaces or on a 30-foot long line leash until the dog's recall is reliable enough to safely grant him off-leash privileges.

Chapter 8

Screening and Pack Composition

Your job will be much easier and more enjoyable if you carefully screen the dogs you walk. This is true of any dog walking situation, but particularly important when walking groups. You want dogs who are compatible with one another, with the terrain you walk, and with the kinds of animals, people, and experiences you're likely to encounter there. You want dogs who are compatible with your skill level and that match your personality. Just because we're dog lovers doesn't mean we enjoy the company of all dogs we meet. And each of us has certain dog behaviors that are low on our charm list. Be sure you truly enjoy the dogs you take out into the world—they'll have more fun and you will, too.

Screening

Ultimately, screening is about safety as well. Make decisions about each dog that are in that dog's interest and the interest of any dogs she'll be walking with, as well as dogs and people you may encounter.

There's one critical question up front: how long have the clients known the dog? If she has just been adopted recently, the clients' information will be much less reliable. For one, they don't have much of a history with the dog, so their data set is weak. For another, the dog may still be adjusting to her new home. Dogs often shut down when in a new environment. This is particularly common of dogs coming from shelters. It may be several weeks, even a month or two, before the dog relaxes enough to express who she really is.

In these situations, it's not a bad idea to play it safe for all concerned—you, the dog, and the clients—by suggesting to the family that they let their new member settle in for a few weeks before sending her out with a dog walker, particularly in group situations.

There are four categories of screening information: demographics, dog-dog interactions, dog-people interactions, and training and general behavior.

Demographic information

Sex, age, size, breed
To begin with, this category includes the basics—sex, age, size, and breed.

Why do you need it?
To help you choose dogs who fit well together. Remember, for example, the 50% size rule that keeps dogs safe from predatory drift incidents. Think about whether you enjoy the company of male or female dogs more, or prefer a balance. Ask yourself whether that senior in your pack really wants an adolescent Lab constantly hassling her to play. Matching dogs based on their basic demographics can increase their enjoyment of their walks while making yours easier.

Intact or fixed
We talked about the challenges of walking intact males and females in Chapters 4 and 5, particularly off leash. Are you up for the extra management and risk involved? When discussing this issue with clients, be sure to ask when their dog was altered, as it can take up to six months for testosterone levels to drop in a recently neutered dog.

Why do you need it?
Because intact males are more prone to wandering (for off-leash walking) and they tend to get into a lot of fights when fixed males pick on them. Intact females can draw unwanted males and can sometimes be more aggressive.

Medical issues and food restrictions
Ask about medical issues and allergies, including any treat restrictions. For dogs with severe food allergies, ask the client to put that dog's daily food rations in a baggie for you to dole out on the walk.

Why do you need it?
Knowing about medical issues and what to watch for if any exist will help you notice a problem early. And depending on the issue, you may choose not to take the dog.

Dog-dog information

Socialization history
You may not know the dog's socialization history, particularly if she has come from a shelter or rescue situation. People who have raised their dog from puppyhood, however, should be able to tell you a little bit about the dog's early experiences with other dogs and people. Dogs who were given ample opportunity as puppies to meet other dogs and people and experience the world outside their home and yard are more likely to be good candidates.

Why do you need it?
It gives you some insight into whether the dog is likely to be good with new people, unfamiliar dogs, and new situations.

Play history
How many friends does the dog have? How often does she get to play with her friends? Meet new ones? How often does she get out? What is her play style?

Why do you need it?
This gives you a sense of the data set the client is drawing on when making her assessment of her dog's play and social skills. If the dog plays well with the neighbor's dog, but doesn't really meet many other canines (and never has), the dog won't necessarily be good with a group of dogs.

On-leash interactions
How does the dog respond when she sees another dog while on leash? Does she ignore the dog? Is she happy and excited while pulling to go say hello? Or does she growl, bark, or lunge toward the other dog? If it's the latter, can she be easily refocused?

Why do you need it?
Hopefully this is obvious. You need to know whether the dog will be able to walk calmly down the street and encounter dogs, or whether you will have to actively scan the environment, being ready to cross the street or duck behind a parked car (and you need to decide whether you're willing to do that). Or, if you have the skill set, whether you're willing to take on the training challenge.

Resource guarding
(For dogs who will be walked in groups.) Does the dog have trouble sharing toys like tennis balls or sticks with fellow canines? Will she

be likely to get into a scuffle if you accidentally drop a treat on the ground? Will there be fireworks at the water bowl?

Why do you need it?
In groups, it's important to know about any resource guarders in order to control the trigger resources that are likely to cause scuffles.

Fight and bite history
What sorts of scuffles has she been in? What were the circumstances? What were the fights over? Are there any similarities among the dogs she has fought with (i.e., is it always dogs of a certain sex, breed, or personality type)? What has been the worst damage done, if any?

Why do you need it?
First, you want to know if you've got a dog on your hands who's engaging in more than a normal, acceptable number of scuffles, so you can avoid including that dog in group situations. It's perfectly normal for an adult dog to have been in a few scuffles, but it's helpful to know what those scuffles were over so you can avoid known triggers or situations. It's also helpful to know when this dog gets into a fight whether she's likely to cause damage.

In some ways, it's a safer bet to walk a dog who has been in a couple of fights but never done any real damage than a dog who has never been in a scuffle. Odds are that some day she will and when it happens, you won't know what to expect. Will she leave spit trails or send the other dog to the emergency room?

Dog-people information

Reaction to strangers
What happens when she encounters a new person? Is this true of all people? What about men versus women, different ethnicities, "strange" pictures, children? Is her reaction different on leash versus off?

Why do you need it?
Another obvious one. You put the dog, yourself, and the client at risk if you take a people reactive dog out into the world.

Movement sensitivity
How does she react to people on the move—bicycles, skateboards, joggers, etc? Does she ignore them? Does she show interest but is easily refocused? Does she bark or lunge at them?

Why do you need it?
Though dogs who lunge at bicycles and joggers don't typically do so out of aggression (it could be just the thrill of the chase or herding behavior), this behavior still frightens people and can still cause injury. But if you know, you can scan the environment for the dog's trigger objects and be ready to distract her and keep her close—or decide that it's not a risk you're comfortable with.

Resource guarding (from people)
(For dogs walked individually and in groups.) Is she likely to let you take a ball? What if she picks up something potentially dangerous like a dead bird or rodent? Will she let you take it from her mouth? Does she have a drop cue?

Why do you need it?
As a dog walker there will be times where you need to be able to take something from a dog, and you need to know whether you can do that safely.

Handleability
Will she have any trouble letting you reach for her collar to clip and unclip the leash? Will you be able to wipe her paws after a muddy trail, check her fur for ticks and burrs, pick her up should she need to be lifted for any reason?

Why do you need it?
It's very difficult to walk a dog without touching her. Any dog you walk needs to allow you to hold her collar, bend over her, wipe her body down with a towel, and possibly lift her in and out of a car.

Bite history
Have there been any bites to people? What were the circumstances, and what was the nature of any damage?

Why do you need it?
You need to know what types of interactions with what types of people might trigger a bite, so you can decide whether you can safely avoid those situations or whether the dog is too risky to walk. Again, remember that you put yourself, the dog, and the client at risk when walking dogs with known bite histories. (Though one way to safely walk a dog with a bite history is to teach the dog to love wearing a muzzle.)

Training and general behavior information

Training history

Does she have a particular cue or behavior that's very reliable? Has she done any training classes or private training and, if so, what kind?

Why do you need it?

It's helpful to know what training experiences a dog has had. First, if the dog has a strong cue she responds to reliably, you can use that to get and maintain her attention in distracting situations. Second, a dog who has been through compulsion-based classes or private training is often nervous about training. It might be easier to choose new cues to build behaviors you need from scratch so she can relax and respond more easily.

Recall

For on-leash walks, you likely won't even ask about recall, but it's the biggie for anyone walking dogs off leash. You should probably assume that most dogs don't have a particularly reliable recall. That's okay, because we can fix that. (Refer back to Chapter 7.)

Why do you need it?

The stronger the recall, the safer the dog and the easier your job.

Leash manners

Of particular interest for on-leash walkers. Pulling is not so bad, as it can be easily addressed with a myriad of humane anti-pull devices. But there's also stalling (when dogs dig in their heels and refuse to move forward), crisscrossing (where dogs constantly move to the left and right, or even circle behind their walker), and biting the leash (a typically unwelcome form of tug-of-war that may be fun for the dog but is worth a trip to the chiropractor for the walker). These leash behaviors will require some work to retrain.

Why do you need it?

Again, the more polite and easy-to-walk the dog is on leash, the more enjoyable your job will be and the less money you'll be spending on massage to work the kinks out of your back. And in group situations it's imperative that dogs can walk politely on leash.

Motivators

What does this dog really like? A particular type of treat? Anything she can eat? Or are tennis balls king? Maybe a good stick or being asked to do her favorite trick?

Why do you need it?
Knowing what motivates a dog gives you tremendous ability to keep her focused and safe.

Car manners
If you'll be transporting the dog, find out what she's like in the car. Does she whine excitedly the whole trip? Bark at dogs and passersby? Get car sick? Can she be crated? Will she share space with another dog comfortably?

Why do you need it?
Some dog walkers never put dogs in cars, and if that will be you, you don't need this. But if you'll be transporting dogs as part of your walking service, you'll be spending a great deal of time with them confined in that small space. Your day will be much more enjoyable if that time is spent with dogs who travel calmly. For group walkers, there's the additional issue of making sure you can transport the dogs together safely without incident.

Scavenging and rolling
What is the dog likely to do when she encounters animal feces or carcasses or other strong-smelling items? Some sniff, pee, and move on. Others will consume such doggie delicacies. And then there are the shoulder divers—those who roll in the muck with glee.

Why do you need it?
You want to know if you have a dog on your hands who regularly eats things that make her sick. If you do, you'll need to manage that either through careful awareness of the environment and a strong recall or by teaching the dog to wear a muzzle to protect her from her own impulses—and to avoid a vet trip and an unhappy client. As for rolling, you're either taking a side trip to the nearest doggie wash or risking an unamused client returning home to a muck-encrusted dog.

Prey drive
If you walk in an area where you're likely to encounter small animals like bunnies, squirrels, etc., it's good to know if you've got a dog who will give chase. You may also need to share trail space with horses on occasion, or even turn a corner to find a field of cows. Your clients may not have taken their dogs into these situations, but if they have it's nice to know how the dog responded. For urban leash walks, squirrels and cats will be the most common prey trigger. Does the dog take notice and then move on, or is she the type to put on a full noise and scrambling display as you drag her away? Of most concern

for these dogs is walking in a group, as the excitement can trigger redirected aggression among the dogs themselves in their frustration at not being able to get to the prey animal.

Why do you need it?

For on-leash dog walkers, an active prey drive means having your shoulder pulled out of the socket every time a squirrel or a bird whips by. And off-leash dogs with high prey drive are more likely to run off and be less responsive to recalls.

Pack composition

Best pack candidates

For those of you walking groups of dogs, your best candidates are likely to be dogs who are generally social with other dogs and people. They don't have to love playing with every dog they meet. They don't even have to love playing at all. But they should be comfortable with other dogs and when encountering new dogs and people.

If you will be walking dogs off leash, they should ideally be food-motivated. Toy-motivation is a bonus, as it's great to have multiple ways to get dogs' attention, keep it, and reward it. A strong recall and obedience training helps, too.

Worst pack candidates

Unless you have specialized skills, avoid walking dogs with dog-dog and dog-people reactivity or aggression issues. Take long-term back-yard dogs with caution, as they have likely been poorly socialized and may fall into this category. Watch their behavior around dogs and people carefully.

Dogs with poor play styles will be poor candidates for group walks, particularly those who fall into the Tarzan and bully categories. (Though some Tarzans may be able to handle on-leash groups if their only difficulty is greeting.) Also avoid taking resource guarders in groups unless they only guard resources you can control. For example, a ball guarder should be fine in a group leash walk, as you'll not likely be throwing tennis balls. And you could take a ball guarder in an off-leash group so long as you aren't walking in a place where you're likely to encounter other dogs playing with balls.

Off-leash walkers may want to avoid walking unaltered dogs because of the additional management and risk they bring.

Best pack compositions

Though each walker will have her own preferences, groups comprising varied ages and a mix of sexes, with the majority being older, will generally be the easiest to manage. Take one or two project dogs at most, with the rest being social, so your focus isn't split among too many concerns. And, of course, keep dogs as close to the same size as possible for their safety. Finally, the smaller the group, the safer and easier the group.

Worst pack compositions

Multiple project dogs will always make a group more difficult to manage, and you should consider any intact dog a project dog. A high percentage of adolescents (approximately seven months to one or two years, this varies by breed and individual) will also keep you working harder. And mixing those teenagers with seniors will likely mean lots of effort spent keeping the "kids" out of the seniors' hair.

For safety, once again, avoid a high size differential between dogs in your pack.

Who will you choose?

Now it's time to think about your own preferences. With these safety guidelines and general suggestions in mind, who do you like to walk? What kinds of walks do you like to take? And where will you be walking? Your choices might be different if you're walking a single dog on leash in a suburban neighborhood than if you're walking six dogs off leash on a busy beach. And they might be different still if you're walking the same number of dogs off leash on a quiet trail.

Good screening and pack composition require thinking about personal preferences (do you like an ambling stroll with a group of seniors or do you find that dull? Perhaps you're the type to enjoy the challenge of a group of adolescents or maybe that thought sends you running for a simple desk job?), your own skill sets (do you have the experience and knowledge to handle a dog with dog-people fear issues, for example?), and the challenges of your walking environment (what will you encounter there? How often will you have to pass strangers? Will there be other off-leash dogs present? Prey animals to contend with?).

All this is to say that you, the dog pro, get to decide what type of clients—dog and human—you work with. Speaking of human clients, let's tackle that next.

Chapter 9

Client Intake

Now that you know what kinds of dogs you're looking for, it's time to work with potential clients to learn about their dogs and whether they're the right fit for you—and you for them. The intake process has three steps:

1. Phone or email screen

2. In-person intake interview

3. Trial walk and/or trial period

Phone or email screen

This initial screening opportunity should focus on the most critical information. That means any information that will determine by itself whether or not you take the dog. For example, if you don't walk intact dogs, you'll want to ask that question before you take your time and the clients' in an in-person interview. This isn't time for a full interview, however—ask just the questions whose answers will result in an automatic no. You'll want the basic demographic information about the dog—age, sex, breed, size—particularly if you are walking dogs in a group.

Don't forget to ask for geographical location up front; no point in engaging in a full conversation if the person is outside your service area

While your first contact from a potential client may often come via email, it's not a bad idea to talk with a potential client by phone before going to his home for an in-person interview. This will give you a sense of the client and whether he might be a good personality fit. It's also important for reasons of safety, particularly if you go to your interviews alone.

In-person intake interview

Armed with questions that cover the range of screening issues discussed in Chapter 8, the intake interview most often takes place in the client's home. You may choose for reasons of safety to meet in a neutral location. If so, you'll want to arrange for a space in which you can also meet the dog. Open-air locations such as parks can be tricky from the perspective of the interview, though they give you a better sense of the dog's behavior outdoors. For a more controlled interview venue, consider renting space from a training facility that is not in use during the day or a daycare with empty office space in the evenings.

The purpose of the intake interview is to screen both the dog and the human clients for compatibility with your business. Are the clients people you feel comfortable interacting with? Do they give you a sense that they listen to and respect your policies and services? Is there a reasonable personality match? Is the dog a good fit for your skill set and your walking program? If you're a group walker, does the dog seem likely to fit with your group?

While your goal is to answer these questions as best you can, the client's goal is usually to get you to say yes. Although a few clients will interview you as closely as you interview them, in most cases, by the time the clients have agreed to an intake interview, they're already sold on you. They've perhaps encountered some of your clever marketing or have been given a strong referral from a friend or trusted professional resource. They've followed this lead to your website and been impressed with what they saw. They decided you're the one for them and their dog. Now they want to make the best impression they can.

On top of this desire to get you to say yes, clients often feel anxious about being judged. They may worry their dog's poor recall will disqualify them from your service. They might be embarrassed that their dog pulls on leash. If you stop to think about it, we all feel on some level that our dog's behavior reflects on us. These feelings may lead some clients, whether consciously or not, to share misleading information about their dog's behavior.

Further complicating this situation, most dog owners are at the mercy of misleading conventional wisdom about dogs and may misinterpret some of their dog's behaviors. It's not uncommon to encounter dog owners who laugh off serious behavior problems, not recognizing them for what they are, just as it's not uncommon for some people to worry needlessly over behaviors that are not at all serious.

For all these reasons, the way you ask questions is important. How you ask a question often determines the usefulness of the information you receive. Here are some tips:

1. Put clients at ease
Start the interview by telling clients what you're going to be doing and why, in as friendly and comforting a manner as possible. For example:

"Thank you for making the time to meet with me. I have a number of questions to ask you about Charley. I hope it won't feel like the Grand Inquisition! I ask a lot of questions because it's my job to keep Charley safe and make sure he has a great time while out with me. So I want to know everything about him so I can take the best possible care of him." If you're a group walker, you also want to know all about Charley so you can choose the best pack mates for him.

This explanation takes a bit of the anxiety out of the equation for the clients—you're asking questions not to judge them or Charley, but so you learn all his quirks in order to keep him safe and having a good time. The implication is that there are not necessarily right or wrong answers, which means you're likely to get more honest information.

2. Use lay language
You need to know if the dog is a resource guarder. But the client may not know that term, and it may sound serious and negative to lay ears. Rather than asking whether Charley guards toys, try asking what he does when another dog would like to share a favorite toy of his. Everyone understands what sharing means, and the language is much less packed with judgment.

3. Ask open-ended, not yes or no, questions
Most behavior is not black or white, and yes/no questions don't leave room for the maybe situations in between. They also don't provide nearly as much information as a narrative answer. You can ask, "Does your dog like meeting other dogs when on leash?" for example. But what does it mean if a client says "yes"? It means only that she thinks her dog is okay meeting other dogs on leash. But she's not a professional, and you are left with no information about how the dog behaves in that situation.

4. Ask questions that seek description, not interpretation

When screening a new dog, you want to know what the dog does in specific situations. The clients' interpretation of their dog's behavior is interesting, but not useful for determining what he's likely to do when you next encounter an unknown dog or a child. And remember—the clients may well not understand what they're seeing.

So rather than asking questions such as "Does your dog like meeting other dogs when on leash?" try "What does your dog do when he meets a new dog when you're walking him on leash?" The "What does your dog do when…" construction encourages potential clients to describe what they've actually seen happen rather than tell you their belief about what their dog's behavior means. If clients give you an interpretive answer, such as "He gets really happy," follow up with a question that forces description: "What does he do that shows you he's happy?" or "Describe what he does to show he's happy about meeting a new dog."

This one trick can make a huge difference in the quality and reliability of the information you gather at your intake interviews.

Trial walk and/or trial period

If everything sounds good after the intake interview and you have a spot for Charley in your schedule or pack, it's time to try him out. Depending on your situation, you may agree to take Charley on, contingent on a short trial period to make sure he's enjoying himself and is a good fit with the rest of your group. In some situations you may feel more comfortable taking Charley on a trial walk first. When walking in groups, you might wish to try him with just one or two other very social dogs before incorporating him into the larger group. If he needs a lot of training work or you feel the need to establish a bit more rapport with him before caring for him in a group setting, it may be appropriate to walk him separately for a week or two before adding him in with the rest of your pack.

Either way, if you walk dogs off leash, be sure to walk any new charges on a long line until you've built enough rapport and recall reliability to allow for off-leash safety.

Chapter 10

Good Business Practices

Legal requirements

At the time of writing, dog walking is a largely unregulated industry. You will, however, need a business license from your city and a fictitious business name statement from your county clerk's office. (This is sometimes referred to as a doing business as [DBA] statement or an assumed business name [ABN] statement.) In most cases you can download these applications and instructions from your city's and county clerk's websites, and often you can apply online.

Though the industry is unregulated on the state and national level, some local areas are beginning to pass regulations for professional walkers. Check with your city and your local park district about trail and park usage rules, restrictions on the number of dogs you may walk at once, and any permits dog walkers may need to carry.

Pack size

Even if there are no rules governing pack size in your area, keep your groups small for maximum safety for the dogs, the public, and yourself. The fewer dogs you have, the more control you have. The fewer dogs you have, the less likely something is to go wrong. And if something does go wrong, you have fewer dogs to manage during the crisis.

Service options

In most of the country, on-leash walking is the norm. This is largely due to the lack of legal off-leash areas in most places. The majority of walkers walk a single dog at a time, on leash. This service provides maximum attention to and safety for each dog. On the downside, the ratio of driving to walking time is higher and walkers are paid for only one dog at a time. Generally this means lower gross revenue.

The exception, however, is for walkers who have the training skills to specialize in taking on difficult dogs other walkers aren't willing to handle, such as dogs with reactivity toward dogs and/or strangers.

On-leash group walks are common in many big-city urban areas. And thus the popular images on greeting cards and the Internet of a walker with multiple leashed dogs happily treading down a busy city sidewalk together. This style of walking allows for better income, as the walker is paid for multiple dogs at once. It does, though, require a bit of careful dog juggling as you pick up each dog to add him or her to the group. Because it's unsafe to leave dogs tied up in public, the dogs you take on for this service will have to be comfortable with you showing up at their door with their buddies in tow. Dogs who are walked in on-leash groups must also be comfortable with a great deal of close proximity to other dogs over a long duration of time.

Off-leash romps are more popular in the Western states in areas with legal off-leash parks, trails, and beaches. The mecca for this style of walking is the San Francisco Bay Area, where walkers most often take small groups off leash together. This can be financially lucrative and affords by far the most exercise and fun for the dogs, but requires a great deal of skill on the part of the walker. In some areas, off-leash walking is more commonly restricted to one dog at a time, or to dogs from a single household, or to enclosed dog parks. We advise using dog parks only when no other options exist, as they can be high-pressure experiences for many dogs. (Remember that proximity and duration are key factors in dog spats, and dog parks can force both in abundance.) Walkers who take dogs to enclosed spaces will need to take greater-than-usual care to screen for dogs who actively enjoy the prolonged company of other dogs, and who are laid back about meeting new canine and human friends.

Inclement weather services

Dog walkers are a bit like mail carriers—you must work through rain, sleet, and snow. But some weather isn't safe for dogs to walk in. If you live in an area with hard winters or hot summers, it's good to have plans for inclement weather. Without them, you'll experience significant revenue loss when clients decide it's too cold or too hot for Fluffy to go out with you.

Start by discussing guidelines with local vets. Not only will this give you rules to live by (specific temperatures or conditions that trigger your inclement weather services), it's a great chance to network with potential referral sources.

Then let clients know, as part of your service agreement and discussions during the intake interview, what will happen when the weather turns harsh. Plan to visit each dog for some indoor time and to leave mental stimulation toys to occupy them for the afternoon. If you walk dogs individually, you'll be able to spend the same amount of time with them as usual. You'll just spend it indoors (other than a quick potty break), playing high-energy games like indoor recall, tug-of-war, fetch, and hide-and-seek. If you're a group walker, you won't be able to give each dog his full regular hour, but you'll be coming by to get him out for a potty break, spend a little time playing high-energy games, and leave him with a collection of mental stimulation toys to tucker him out.

In addition to stuffed Kongs (trying freezing them the night before to make them last extra long), various treat balls that dispense kibble as the dog rolls them about, and other toys designed to make dogs work and chew to get at the good stuff inside, there are also puzzle toys that require dogs to solve problems in order to access treats. These can help a dog pass a dreary afternoon quite pleasantly, and wear him out good, too. See the Resources section for ideas.

Setting rates

Setting your rates is relatively easy. Take a look around at what other dog walkers in your area are charging. You'll likely find a range. Set your rate at the top of the range. You may be tempted to start lower, but this is a mistake. The range generally represents a picture of local walking rates over time, with the lower rates belonging to dog walkers who have failed to keep their rates current and the higher prices reflecting the current going rate. Starting at the lower end because you're new or want to get a good start means leaving money on the table and starting out behind, with the specter of a large rate increase looming in the future.

You should also aim high because you're looking for good clients—dog lovers who see their dogs as part of the family and want to do right by them. You want people who can easily afford your service and who chose you because they feel you're the best walker for their dog. Do your job well and these people will remain loyal to you for the life of their dog. You don't want the bargain hunters; they'll jump ship as soon as they see another walker charging less.

If you're offering a specialized service, such as walking reactive dogs or offering individual walks in an area where group outings are the norm, charge above the top going rate.

Keep your rates simple

Have one rate for everyone using the same service. Many dog walking businesses create needlessly complicated rate cards based on the number of walks per week. Your clients should choose the number of walks per week based on the number they need—not on whether they get a small discount. And you can only walk a limited number of dogs per day; dog walking is not a volume-based business. It's easy to lose several thousands of dollars a year to such discounts. If you're considering offering a volume discount, I urge you to run the numbers to understand how much money you'll lose by doing so.

Keep your rates current

Review local rates yearly, and plan to increase yours incrementally every one to two years. It's much easier to increase by one or two dollars occasionally than to wait multiple years and find you're five or more dollars behind the times.

Already behind? It's a tough situation to be in, but not unfixable. First determine what your rate should actually be. If you're only down by a dollar or two per walk, you should be able to raise your rates in one step. But if you're down by three or more dollars per walk, consider doing the raise in stages so your clients don't feel the pinch all at once. Separate phases by at least six months. So, for example, you might raise your rates by $3 by instituting a $1.50 raise now and another $1.50 dollars in six months. You would communicate the entire plan to clients at the outset, letting them know you're going to break it up to lessen the immediate impact. If you're terribly behind, you may need to break your increase into three phases to stretch it over a year, or even longer.

Communicating a rate change

Give your clients a written letter explaining the rate change and the reasons behind it. Put a marketing spin on your rate increase. For example, explain how the rate increase allows you to continue your commitment to small walking groups—something you know your clients value. Don't over-apologize. Apologizing profusely and encouraging people to "call if you have any concerns" suggests there's a reason clients should be upset. Always give clients at least a full month's notice before their bill actually increases. Two months' notice is even better.

Good policies are a good policy

Policies are an area where many dog walking companies go wrong. And mistakes in this area of your business usually mean the loss of money—often in the tens of thousands of dollars a year. So set policies carefully and, if you're just getting started, make sure they are policies you can grow into.

Geographical range

Setting tight geographical boundaries for your service area can make all the difference in whether you enjoy the work for the long haul. Ideally you want to spend more time walking dogs and less driving. You'll likely be tempted to break your rules on range when you're just starting out. Don't. You'll rationalize that taking a dog who lives 30 minutes outside of your zone will be good hands-on experience, that you'll just let the client go when you get busy, that it's a nice drive without too much traffic. But unless taking this client literally means the difference between eating or not, ignore these thoughts and take a pass. It's not worth it. You may fall in love with the dog and not want to let him go. You may feel obligated to stick by the client. But the drive will make your days much harder as you become busy, and that will influence your work and how you feel about it. This is an excellent example of setting your policies now—and following them—as though you are already as busy and successful as you intend to be.

Minimum and set days

Don't make the mistake of setting up a drop-in dog walking service. With very few exceptions, you will be much better off selling your service as an ongoing, regular part of your two- and four-legged clients' lives. Require your clients to send their dogs out with you every week, at least twice a week (more is better!), and on the same days each week. You, your clients, and their dogs will all benefit.

Requiring set days provides you a predictable schedule and reliable income. It reduces the administrative hassles of taking weekly and/or last minute walking reservations. It also makes your walks easier. Dogs who don't get out often enough tend to be squirrely and over-hyper. Dogs who walk with you regularly learn to fall into your routine. If you're a group walker, you're able to create consistent groups, knowing that the dogs in each are a good match for each other. And consider this: when you structure your service this way, you need far fewer clients to fill your schedule, making your administrative and marketing duties that much easier.

The clients and dogs benefit, too. A tired dog is a good dog. The more often a dog goes out with a professional walker for exercise, the more likely his people will notice a positive change in his behavior at home, and calm, well-behaved dogs are likely to be treated better. And with set days, your clients always know their spot is reserved. They never need to hassle with weekly reservations or worry about a day they need being full.

This system won't work for all clients. Doctors, for example, don't always have set schedules they can plan around, and may not want to send their dogs out on days they're off. That's okay. You're probably not the only dog walker in your area—pass people who don't fit into your service on to colleagues. That karma will come back to you, and you won't be the one running around each week trying to accommodate a constantly shifting schedule.

If, however, you live in an area where the majority of potential clients have unpredictable or rotating schedules, you may have to adjust your policies. For example, one of our Dog Walking Academy grads lives in a city dominated by three large hospitals. Accordingly, we advised her to keep the minimum number of days rule but let go of the set days requirement. Her hospital workers get their work schedules twice each month, so they commit to set days for two weeks at a time.

Cancellation

Without a strong cancellation policy, you can't accurately predict your income. Walkers without solid cancellation policies often find themselves in sudden financial binds when clients spring news of vacations, business trips, or a decision to work a few days at home. And, of course, when it rains, it pours—you rarely get one of these announcements at a time.

A cancellation policy only works if it protects you from losing money. So if you've asked clients to give you 24 hours notice—or 48 or a full week—your policy probably isn't doing what it should for you. Because if you can't fill a cancelled spot, you lose the money—no matter how much notice a client gives.

We recommend replacing toothless cancellation policies with strong vacation policies. The idea is to limit the number of days a dog can be pulled from your schedule without paying. For example, you might give each client two weeks of vacation time or what one of our grads calls "excused absences." Under this policy, if a client uses your service three days per week, he gets six free days per year. Or you might give clients a certain number of days per month or per quarter. Once they have used their vacation days, they pay for any additional days their dog is out of your rotation.

Offering excused or vacation days acknowledges that life happens, while still protecting your financial viability. You limit the effect clients' lives have on your bottom line. Clients benefit, too, because they know their spot will still be there for them when they get back.

This is not such an unusual idea. Most daycares and private schools for children require payment for each term. If a parent decides to take her five-year-old to Grandma's for a couple of weeks, she doesn't get refunded or credited for that missed time. There may have been space for 20 children in that classroom. She took a spot for her child, and it's hers to pay for whether she uses it or not. If a parent sends his 18-year-old to Harvard and she decides to skip a few classes, Dad won't be seeing a refund or credit, either. Again, he's paying for a space at that institution, regardless of how well his daughter uses it. Same with a gym membership—the monthly fee allows daily access. But though most gym members only manage to get there a couple of times a month, the bill doesn't change.

These businesses run this way because they understand that in order to provide space to a relatively small number of people, they must ask those customers to make a commitment. If part of your goal is to be financially stable, you, too, must ask clients to make a commitment. You don't need many clients, but you do need clients who respect the service you offer and who intend to use it regularly.

Payment
If you're offering a regular service, there's no need for pay as you go. Bill your clients monthly. The best policy is to bill clients at the end of each month for the upcoming one—this is most consistent with the notion of asking clients to commit to a spot for their dog in your walking schedule or groups.

Client communication
As you take care of the dogs each day, it's easy to forget that your clients are actually the humans these dogs live with. It's the human client who cuts your check—and who decides whether or not to keep doing so. It's an odd quirk of this business that we rarely see

our actual clients in person. It means that to build strong and lasting brand loyalty, you need to find other ways to communicate regularly with your human clients. You need to remind them you're there, and remind them what you do for them every day. Because someday you're going to need to raise your rates, or tell them about an accident on the trail. You don't want the only time clients hear from you to be these moments. Besides, providing good customer service is part of being a dog pro—and it feels good, too.

Communicate daily

Let your clients know how their dog's walk went every day. Just a few short notes to say all went well, to share a fun route you took, or a quick cute anecdote. Choose a method of delivery that works well for you—it could be a branded, handwritten note left on the kitchen counter, an email or text, or a voicemail for them to come home to. Providing pictures and even videos of their dog out having fun with you is a great idea as well. There are also new options available these days, such as the Veriwalk app, which allows clients to view the walking route you took, and when you took it. This can be a fun feature to offer your clients, and one that provides them extra peace of mind.

These daily communications keep you in the forefront of your clients' minds. They provide clients a better sense of what happens each day while they're at work, of the fun their dog is having, the care she's being watched with. Ultimately, you're selling peace of mind and relief from guilt to people whose lives are over-full. When they get your bill each month, you want them fully aware of all you do for them.

Communicate seasonally

In addition to the personal daily notes, write your clients a professional letter each quarter in which you share any seasonal notes and communicate any upcoming changes such as rate increases, policy changes, etc. Seasonal notes might include reminding clients of how your inclement weather services work, letting clients know you're heading into tick season and what to watch for, listing any holidays for the coming quarter, even sharing a new dog treat recipe you've found.

Sending these letters out regularly, in addition to your daily communications, builds plenty of padding for when you occasionally have to drop bad news like a rate increase. They also demonstrate your professionalism and the care with which you do your work.

Communicate changes early

When it's time to raise rates or make a policy adjustment or let clients know you'll be going on vacation yourself, give plenty of notice. Rate and policy changes should be communicated at least a full month in advance, and vacations even further out if you can. Be sure to remind clients of an upcoming vacation as the date moves closer, too. You can use your daily notes to do this.

Communicate problems early

If you notice an emerging physical or behavioral problem—even if it seems slight or you're not sure—communicate it right away. Don't wait for possible issues to become full-blown ones before you let a client know about them. A client who's surprised by a problem in full swing is much more likely to have a negative reaction than one who's had plenty of warning something might be going on. And catching issues early makes them easier to head off. Notice a slight limp or change in a dog's gait? A change in appetite or energy level? A change in interest in other dogs? An emerging reticence to share balls with friends or some low growling as other dogs pass? Tell your client right away, let him know you're going to keep an eye on it, and ask him to do the same and report anything he notices. Don't be shy about suggesting a trip to the vet or giving a referral to a positive trainer.

Hiring

Pondering the plunge into hiring staff is often a good sign of your business's health. But growth can be stressful, particularly when it involves taxes and paperwork. Compared to the IRS, dogs are easy to understand. Many first-time employers are tempted to go the independent contractor (IC) route instead of hiring employees, having heard it's easier and cheaper. Maybe you have dog pro peers using ICs. Just make sure you know the implications of your choice, as the legal consequences carry weight.

Emplyees versus independent contractor

Employees are considered official, long-term hires, and they come at a higher cost, as you are responsible for half their Social Security and FICA taxes, as well as payroll taxes, not to mention worker's compensation insurance. So a $10/hour-employee will cost you more than $10/hour. How much more depends on a number of factors, including your location, but you can estimate that an employee will cost approximately an additional 11-12% of the hourly rate you offer.

All this tax and insurance business requires more paperwork, too, though it's probably not as complicated as you fear once the initial set up is completed, and there are tax pros and payroll services to help. (See the Resources section.) In some states, local laws make it more difficult to fire an employee than an independent contractor. This varies considerably state by state, so it's worth your time to research or ask an expert. With these added costs and complexities, however, come some significant benefits. You can train an employee in the style and procedures you prefer. If desired, you can also require that your employees not work for a competitor.

Independent contractors are a different animal altogether. ICs are simpler and less expensive to hire. There's much less paperwork involved and you pay no taxes or workman's comp: $10/hour is $10/hour. Unfortunately, the IRS would prefer you not hire them. They get less money when you hire an IC, and it's easier to commit tax evasion, payment-under-the-table being the most common method. To discourage use of ICs, the IRS uses a very narrow definition of what constitutes an independent contractor.

The chief thing to understand is that an IC must be a professional who owns his own licensed business, and who contracts only a portion of his time to you. He's free to contract the rest of his time to other businesses, including your competition, and to the public as well—which means that he must remain free to compete directly with you. And that's only the beginning. Here are other rules dog walking business owners will have difficulty not breaking:

- You can't train ICs; they should be professionals in their own right, fully formed and skilled at the job they have been hired for.

- You can't provide ICs with materials for the job. Which means walkers have to bring their own leashes, treats, collars, etc.

- Their term of employment should be finite, not ongoing.

- They should not be doing work that is your primary source of revenue. If you run a dog walking business, this means no independent contractors to walk dogs!

This is only a sampling of the IRS's rules of engagement; there are nearly 20. And you only have to break one to be found guilty of misclassifying a worker. In short, there's almost no way for a dog pro to legally hire an independent contractor to provide services for dogs.

Which doesn't mean the desire to go the IC route isn't understandable. And chances are you know other dog pros using ICs. But pointing at the groomer down the street when the IRS comes for you won't get you far; the IRS makes it very clear that claiming precedent doesn't fly.

If you get caught

If you're audited, the IRS will likely demand the taxes you would have paid had your IC been an employee, as well as interest owed on those taxes. Not to mention a probable fine. A little math will tell you that the longer you used an IC illegally, the more you'll owe Uncle Sam.

Will I get caught?

Statistically speaking, you aren't likely to be audited. But paying money to the same ICs year after year could get you flagged, particularly if the sums are equivalent to local salaries. You could also land on the IRS's radar if an IC files a complaint against you with the Department of Labor. Again, the odds are against exposure. But if you do get caught, the results could be catastrophic; I know of dog pros who were pushed into bankruptcy and lost their businesses (which, by the way, won't pardon those taxes).

Boy, am I in trouble

If your stomach has been sinking as you read these words, no need to panic. What's done is done, and now you know. If your use of ICs has fallen outside of legal boundaries, there's no time like the present to bring your ICs on as official hires. The longer you wait, the steeper the potential costs. So take the leap into full-on employment. Yes, you'll pay a little more, but consider it money well spent for a good night's sleep and the benefits that come with employees.

But I'm not ready

If you've yet to hire anyone for anything, and/or are still uncertain about taking on a full employee, consider these alternatives:

- Hire an independent contractor for a short period of time— say, six months—as a trial. If you like him and his work, play it safe by transitioning him into full employment.

- Get creative. Consider an internship program as an alternative—you get assistance and your intern gets valuable job experience and training. This is also a great way to audition potential hires.

- Find professional help for non-business tasks such as child care, housecleaning, and errand running. Help in such areas can free up more of your own time to devote to the business.

What to pay?

There are no real standards in the industry for what or how to pay dog walkers who work for you. Some businesses pay an hourly rate, some pay a flat rate per dog, some pay a percentage of gross revenue for the walk. Each approach has its advantages: an hourly rate makes your overhead predictable, and your employee knows her take-home will be steady. A percentage or flat rate per dog means your overhead is directly proportionate to your revenue, but can cause conflict with employees when their walking routes aren't kept full and their income dips.

Take a look around at the going rate for walkers in your area or, if there aren't many, at how pet sitters are paid. Consider paying better than the going rate in order to attract and keep the best walkers on your team. Turnover can be very disruptive to a service business. Paying well and treating your walkers as valued members of your team, whose input is welcomed, goes a long way in keeping your staff steady. We've also found companies that hire part-time instead of full-time have lower turnover, at least in part because the physical nature of the work and amount of time spent driving can lead to quick burnout. A team of part-time walkers also means easier coverage when a walker calls in sick, twists an ankle, or requests vacation time.

Working for others

If you work for others, remember this one thing: the dogs you walk and the people they live with are not *your* clients; they belong to the company you work for. It's unethical to solicit business away from the company you work for at any time for any reason, including and especially should you decide to move on to work for yourself. I highly commend you for making a choice to go out on your own, and hopefully your employer will cheer and support you as well. But regardless of her reaction, don't begin your new business with an unethical act.

Allow your employer to communicate your departure to the clients whose dogs you've been walking. If a client asks you to take her dog, decline politely and suggest she speak to your employer. Ideally you and your employer will have set up a plan for this moment ahead of time and there will be protocols for handling clients who wish their dog to go with you when you depart. When I help businesses set up their employee agreements I often recommend an arrangement in which a departing employee pays a pre-set fee to the employer for any clients who go with her into her new business. This is a fair win-win-win for all involved: the employee gets a jump start on her business, the employer is compensated for the loss, and the client gets the walker he wants.

Chapter 11

Emergency Planning

Taking care of other people's best friends means living with the chilling prospect of accidents. Out on a trail, an otherwise reliable dog takes off chasing an unknown scent and is lost or hit by a car. Two dogs who normally play well together get into a nasty fight. A dog you are walking swallows a rock or other non-edible item whole. All are scenarios that make dog walkers sweat. But failing to consider and prepare for accidents will only aggravate an already bad situation if it happens. The clients, the dogs, your staff, yourself—everyone is better served by a proactive approach.

In preparation

Always have client contact information on hand
You should never have to rummage frantically through your vehicle for your phone list or, perish the thought, go home to get it. Keep up-to-date, well-organized client contact details in your car at all times, and require any staff to do so as well.

Program emergency vet phone numbers into your phone
Write down emergency directions to the closest vets from your most-used trails or the neighborhoods you service and keep them in any car ever used to transport dogs. Make sure all staff members know where to find the directions and understand them. Even if you work solo and you know the directions well, write them down or have them pre-programmed into your phone or GPS. When a crisis hits, it's all too easy to forget one's own name, let alone how to get to the veterinary hospital.

Recruit an emergency assistant
One way to prevent panic in an emergency is to have a person to call who can help you keep calm and assist with urgent tasks. Don't just

make a mental list of cool-headed friends, though. Your emergency assistant must know and agree to his or her new designation, and the two of you should set up a protocol for such calls. Maybe it's her job to meet you at the vet clinic and provide general support. Maybe she is the one who takes the other dogs home. Maybe she finishes your walking stops for the day. Whatever it is, you always know that someone can come to your aid. You and a fellow dog pro can do this for each other, or you can ask a friend who works from home or has a flexible office schedule.

Take your emergency assistant out with you on your regular rounds so she can meet all the dogs. Then practice your emergency protocol with your assistant to make sure everything goes as planned when you really need it to.

Get it in writing
Your client service contract should clearly spell out what's expected of you in an emergency.

1. Have owners give you permission to seek emergency treatment and agree to cover the cost.

2. Have owners specify whether there's a cap on the cost they will accept. (Don't assume everyone shares your willingness to take out a second mortgage to pay for surgery.)

3. Have owners specify whether they authorize you to take the dog to whichever vet or animal hospital is closest. In other words, they want you to exercise discretion in getting their dog the best, fastest care. Otherwise, they may refuse to pay because you didn't use their vet.

4. Have owners state their wishes with regards to resuscitative care. For example, some clients may not wish to have senior dogs resuscitated.

If it happens

Secure any other dogs in your care
Group walkers with an injured dog on the trail need to secure the other dogs first of all to keep the situation from escalating. The last thing you need while dealing with an injured dog is for another one to take himself off on an adventure. Get everyone safely tethered, then call your emergency assistant.

Communicate with the client

Call the client when you have calmed down, not before. Also hold off until you know the precise nature of the damage. Sprained leg or amputation? Eye patch for a few days or blindness? Best to find out before you make the dreaded call. When you do, speak in a calm, confident tone. A distressed owner needs to know a professional is in charge of the crisis. Clearly state whether everything is handled and this is just a courtesy call to let the client know, or whether some action on her part is required.

With any kind of mishap, even if everything turned out fine, the best policy is to tell the client. Some clients might not care that their dog was missing for 20 minutes on a deer-chasing adventure, or that he got into a scuffle in which no one was hurt, but that risk is preferable to a client who hears it from someone else and is outraged at your failure to tell her about the dramatic event, regardless of the outcome. And if running off or scuffles become a trend, your client may be angry to learn something's been brewing and wonder why you didn't let her know sooner.

What to say

Take responsibility as appropriate—you are an adult and a professional. But don't verbally rub sand in your hair, don't heap blame on yourself, and don't ever tell the client they ought to sue you. Accidents happen. Dogs are not appliances.

Depending on the situation, here is a possible strategy for the conversation: describe in a straightforward manner exactly what happened, share all the steps you took to handle the situation, give a report of the current status of the dog, and share anything you plan to do (if relevant) in the way of policy or process changes to avoid something similar happening in the future. Stress your concern for the dog's and the client's well-being, and ask if there's anything else you can do to be of support at this particular moment.

Follow-up

If the worst happens and a dog is seriously injured or killed while under your care, let your other clients know in writing. Bad news travels fast and if you are not the one to tell them, they may think you're trying to hide the episode. You have to protect your business and your brand, and honesty is the best policy.

The letter should include any policy changes you are making to prevent the same thing happening again. Be thoughtful about protecting anonymity; don't hang clients out to dry. If a dog is expelled, for example, don't name that dog. If a dog is killed, find out whether the owner wants the dog named or not. Some do, some don't. But don't name the dog who killed, just say he was expelled.

Openness is the best policy about smaller incidents, too. A scuffle in a walking group that results in a dog needing a couple of stitches, for example, should also be communicated. Doing so breeds confidence, prevents rumors from festering and growing, and demystifies normal canine behavior. Emphasize what is being done about the problem: "We had another tiff over tennis balls today, so we have decided not to bring them to the beach with us anymore." Hopefully, you are communicating with your clients every week anyway (highlights from Fido's week, etc.), so bad news isn't the only news they get.

(Of course, if scuffles happen more than once in a blue moon, something is wrong. Screening procedures and staff training are the first places to look for a possible issue.)

Don't fret
If you generally run a strong business, if you take good care of dogs and of people, if you handle a crisis with responsibility and grace, it's rare to lose clients over injury incidents. Be open and honest, be calm, and face the situation down—it can happen to anyone.

Chapter 12

Marketing for Dog Walkers

Most dog walkers dabble in marketing. They order business cards, place brochures or rack cards in a few dog businesses, put up a website, place a couple local ads, maybe start a Facebook page, and call it a day. Then they sit and wait, growing increasingly frustrated at how slowly business grows.

This chapter will show you how to go much further with your marketing efforts, even if you're operating on a shoestring budget and the word "marketing" makes your stomach do uncomfortable things.

Why market?

Simply put: because you want to be a dog walker, and to be a dog walker you need clients. Too many dog pros put their faith in a "build it and they will come" approach to marketing, but word of mouth only works once enough people know about you. You'll need to do plenty of marketing before word of mouth kicks in to help out. Without a concerted marketing plan, filling your walking schedule will be a slow process.

What are you marketing?

If you're in a busy market full of fellow dog walkers, you'll need marketing to convince potential clients to choose you over all their other choices. If dog walking is a relatively new concept in your area, your marketing task will be to raise awareness of the service and convince dog lovers they need a dog walker.

Your marketing message

Either way, you need a clear marketing message that focuses on the benefits of your service to your human clients. The human clients part is critical. You'll be tempted to build your website and marketing materials around how great walking is for dogs. This is important to include, but it shouldn't be the primary focus of your marketing message. Dogs don't carry checkbooks, and they lack the opposable thumbs needed to write a check anyway. They won't be the decision makers. (Too bad—running a dog business would be much easier if they were!)

It's the humans you must appeal to. And you can't do that by simply telling them walking is good for dogs and how much their dog will love it. This is all true and certainly has a place. But people make decisions primarily based on their own needs, and part of successful marketing is speaking to those needs.

So why do people hire dog walkers? What's in it for them? Two things: relief from guilt and worry, and a better-behaved dog. Dog owners who work long hours often spend time worrying or feeling badly about the dog they left home alone. And if they don't, part of your job will be convincing them they should. Essentially, you're selling peace of mind here: go to work and focus, knowing all is well at home.

Dog owners who work long hours are less likely to have a well-exercised dog, which means they're more likely to come home to a dog who is hyper and desperate for exercise and attention, and to a house that has suffered the destruction of a bored and lonely dog. A tired dog is more enjoyable to live with. Here you're selling not only relief, but the joy of coming home to a relaxed dog who's content to curl up on the couch for the owners' favorite TV program instead of insisting on a two-hour hike around the neighborhood after a hard day at work.

By all means tell clients how good walking is for the health of their dog, and how much better their dog's life will be with you in it. But that message should take a backseat to the impact hiring a dog walker will have on the clients' quality of life. Remember, they're the ones who will be doing the hiring.

Your professional bio

Your professional bio, whether on the About page of your website or any other marketing materials, should be just that: a professional bio. It's not enough to say that you've grown up with dogs and have been around them all your life, that you have a special dog who led you to work with dogs for a living, or that you love dogs passionately.

For one thing, so does just about every other dog walker out there. For another, potential clients are checking you out to see if you'll be a good fit for them and their dog, not to learn about your childhood or your dogs. They want to know your credentials and business ethics—what makes you qualified, trustworthy? What would it be like to hire you? Why pick you?

Your bio is part of your marketing message. So lead with your credentials: are you a certified dog walker? Have you been working with dogs professionally for a good number of years? Do you read extensively on dog behavior topics? Attend seminars? Belong to professional associations? Then slip in your marketing message: you understand the plight of busy professionals and families, and you enjoy spending the day with clients' dogs so they can spend their days working, caring for their children, or whatever other responsibilities they may have. Close on a more personal note. This is where you can mention your own dogs, interesting hobbies or past careers, even how you got into dog walking. Keep this section short and jaunty; just enough to give people a sense of your personality.

A bio case study

Here's a typical dog pro bio:

"Lisa's love of dogs stems from early childhood when she got her first Border Collie growing up on a ranch in Michigan. But it was Chase, a Border Collie/Aussie mix she adopted in 1997, that introduced her to dog walking. Chase had far too much energy. Lisa hired a trainer to help Chase. The trainer explained that exercise would go a long way toward helping Chase become a more relaxed member of the family. Lisa started taking Chase on long daily walks and noticed a difference in Chase's behavior almost immediately.

That's when Lisa decided to leave her career in accounting to open Best Friends Dog Walking. She now enjoys fulfilling her passion for dogs by getting to walk them every day. Lisa is a member of XYZ and QRS, and has her certification as a professional dog walker from the dog*tec Dog Walking Academy."

This bio isn't terrible, and Lisa comes off as a lovely person. But it's not quite a professional bio. So let's retool it:

"Lisa Smith is a Certified Professional Dog Walker and graduate of the dog*tec Dog Walking Academy. She is a professional member of XYZ and QRS associations. Committed to keeping the dogs in her care safe and having a great time, Lisa is certified in Canine First Aid and avidly pursues ongoing continuing education and professional development by attending several seminars per year and keeping current on all industry literature.

Best Dog puts clients first and is well respected and referred to by local veterinarians, professional dog trainers, and the Our Town SPCA as an ideal way for busy dog owners to get their dogs the exercise they need to be healthy, happy, and easy to live with. When not helping clients to enjoy easier lives with their canine companions, Lisa enjoys taking silly pictures of her own three dogs."

Notice how the first bio is all about Lisa and her personal story, with her professional credentials taking a backseat. Whereas the second bio is about clients and their needs, and Lisa's qualifications to help them meet those needs. Her marketing message is in there, too, with the emphasis about how her service makes clients' lives easier. Lisa's own dogs are mentioned only briefly to add a personal touch. This is a bio that communicates competence, professionalism, and benefits.

Your three marketing audiences

Once you've done some thinking about your marketing message, it's time to think about who that message is for. A complete marketing plan should address three distinct audiences: referral sources, potential clients, and current and past clients.

Referral sources

It's common to think primarily about marketing to the general public—letting all dog owners know you exist. But referral sources—other dog professionals who send clients your way—are the most critical audience as you start out, and they're who will feed your business for long-term sustainability as well. Get a few good referral sources on your side and your business will build more quickly.

Referral sources such as veterinarians, dog daycares, dog trainers, pet sitters, and pet supply stores tend to come into contact with people precisely when they need your services the most. Potential clients may complain to a veterinarian or dog trainer about their dog's destructive or hyperactive behavior, be told by a daycare their dog isn't a good fit for group play, or worry out loud to a pet sitter about an overly long workday. You want these fellow dog pros to have your name on the tip of their tongues when that happens.

Potential clients

Don't confuse marketing to potential clients with marketing to the general public. The more you narrow your focus, the less money and effort you'll need to spend on your marketing, and the more successful returns you'll see.

You really don't want all people with dogs to call you anyway. For one thing, you only want people within your service area. Make that too broad and you'll spend more time driving than walking. And there's no point in marketing your services to people who can't afford them, so socio-economic factors come into play as well. You may wish to further narrow your focus to specific sub-culture groups. For example, perhaps you wish to tailor your message to busy families. Maybe you want to appeal to the green-minded in your community by emphasizing your green dog walking vehicle. Or to the gay community or to churchgoers. It's not necessary to focus your audience in this way, but the more specific you are, the easier it will be to both tailor your message and target your marketing efforts.

Choosing a service niche is another way to tailor your message and narrow your target audience. You might specialize in walking small dogs, or big ones, or those of a specific breed. You might provide a service a bit different from other walkers in your area, for example by offering individual walks when everyone else is walking in groups, or vice versa. Maybe you have a complementary skill set that allows you to put a spin on your service, such as a vet tech background that qualifies you to walk elderly, infirm, or post-injury dogs, or some training expertise that allows you to walk dogs with dog-dog or stranger issues that other walkers won't take on.

Anytime you narrow your focus by targeting a specific audience or declaring a niche, you increase the likelihood of those clients choosing you above all others. It may seem on the surface like a limiting strategy, but your business will grow much faster when you make yourself the obvious choice for a subset of your community.

Current and past clients

Retention marketing is key to longevity. This will be the smallest portion of your marketing plan as you start out, but should grow in importance as your business grows. You'll spend time and resources landing your clients; it makes no sense not to keep them in your marketing loop. This is not just good customer service, it's also how you build word of mouth over time. Get enough happy clients talking and you end up with more happy clients.

What kind of marketing?

Most people think about the obvious things when it's time to market: ads, brochures, business cards. These are all reasonable things to do, but they're the tip of the iceberg and generally the least effective kind of marketing in our industry. This is passive advertising—paying money to declare that you exist and are great. The problem is, most of us do our level best to ignore advertising. We fast-forward past commercials, divert our eyes or click away from ads, and rarely pick up the many brochures waiting for us in various places of business. We're just overloaded with marketing messages; our minds are already full.

The most effective marketing is marketing that doesn't seem like marketing. If you can dress your message up as education and entertainment, it's much more likely to be welcomed by your audiences. This is called community or content marketing. The idea is to give to your community in some way, to share your expertise (your content), to build relationships.

Community marketing has distinct advantages for dog walkers. It tends to be much less expensive than traditional advertising projects.

It also requires much less direct selling of oneself, something many dog pros find distinctly uncomfortable. And it makes great use of your passion for and expertise about dogs. On the flip side, though, it generally demands a larger time commitment. You didn't think you were going to get out of this marketing thing without spending something, right? But the time you spend on your community marketing will bring you far a better return on that investment than the dollars you might have spent on ads or brochures.

Community marketing ideas

Network with referral sources

Let other dog pros know you're there. When a vet tells a client his dog needs more exercise for health reasons, when a trainer suggests exercise to positively affect behavior, when a daycare determines a dog isn't a good fit for a group environment, or a fellow walker turns away a dog for lack of space in her schedule, your name should be the first these dog pros think of.

Networking can be done in a variety of ways. A bold overture and suggestion of mutual referrals is great, but if you're a bit more shy you might try an invitation to coffee. Shyer still? Email to the rescue. But go beyond a simple introduction. The trick to effective networking is to make yourself useful. Join local and national professional email groups and occasionally share information others might appreciate—let colleagues know about a behavior seminar coming to town, for example, and offer to carpool or meet up for lunch. Share a good article link about business success or leash aggression. Pass along a new anti-pull tool or other helpful equipment. In short, be present. Be friendly. Be useful. Don't worry if you hear nothing but silence back at first; just keep at it and you'll eventually develop collegial friendships and see referrals come your way. Be sure to include your website address, service areas, and services in your email signature so people become familiar with what you do. You can share all these emails with local dog pros who aren't on lists, too. Just send an introduction email first telling them about your business and asking about theirs, so they know who you are when you begin sending additional emails.

Create a "Why Hire" poster/flier

Rather than, or at least in addition to, traditional print pieces like brochures or postcards, use a content-rich print piece like a Why

Hire poster or flier. Give it a title like "Why Hire a Professional Dog Walker?" or "5 Things to Ask Your Dog Walker." Give a short number of concise answers or pointers, using clear subheaders, bullet points, or a numbered list, and leaving plenty of white space. Brand the piece with your logo and colors to match your website, and include your website address at the bottom.

Such a piece gets people thinking about the difference between a professional dog walker and an amateur, and about what dog walking can do for them. And if they agree with what you have to say, why would they call someone else?

Write an article

If you're a skilled writer, offer the local paper an article on a day in the life of a dog walker, or the things you've learned from walking other people's dogs. Nothing says "expert" like your name in print, and your article gives you a chance to share your expertise, your professionalism, and your passion for and thoughtfulness about what you do. It's a window into your personality and integrity, a glimpse of what a dog would experience with you, and the peace of mind people stand to gain knowing you're there during the day when they can't be.

If the article goes over well, suggest turning it into a regular column. The only thing better than your name in print is getting it there and in front of potential clients on a regular basis.

Give a lecture

If you're more of a speaker than a writer, take the same approach on the stage—another way to proclaim yourself the local dog walking expert. A multimedia talk with photos and video clips will give people a close look at what a professional dog walker does and what their dogs could be doing instead of chewing the couch. It also gives them a first-hand experience of you.

Approach a local shelter to offer your talk as a fundraiser for them. Charging a nominal donation fee for the shelter means a space to give the talk and a marketing partner to help spread the word and fill seats. You can also approach a boutique pet supply store to suggest a joint event. You get access to their audience, and they get to put on an event that brings people into the store. Suggest they offer a discount on any purchases made the evening or afternoon of your talk.

Distribute a newsletter

Printed newsletters are powerful public marketing because they get your brand and expertise in front of people repetitively. Dog lovers reading your quarterly newsletter begin to develop brand loyalty without even consciously realizing it. If they've enjoyed your tips about making their own walks easier, your recipes for homemade dog biscuits, reviews of the best trails or dog parks, fun facts about dogs through history, and client dog profiles, why would they choose anyone else when it's time to hire a walker?

You can also use your newsletter as a referral marketing tool by including a review of a dog-friendly business or other dog pro in each edition. Why wouldn't the café that allows dogs on the patio, or the vet clinic, or the pet supply store that you feature in your newsletter want to let you leave a few each quarter? Let them know you plan to include a highlight of their business and ask them if they'd like to include a small discount or special for your readers, free of charge. This will be a great opportunity to introduce yourself, when you have something to offer instead of something (i.e., referrals) to ask for. Do for others and the referrals will follow.

Follow the 15% rule for your newsletter content: no more than 15% of the content should be about you or your business. The rest should be educational or entertaining information about dogs. Break this rule and you're likely to produce a glorified brochure rather than a newsletter—and people rarely read brochures more than once.

As with all materials, your newsletter should be clearly branded and include easy-to-find contact information.

Print a calendar

There are a number of great online sources for creating personalized calendars inexpensively.

Print a customized, branded calendar for distribution to your clients, referral sources, and potential clients. (For example, you can offer copies to the local rescue group to send home with adopters and their new dogs.) Feature one or more client dogs on each month of the calendar with a short bio. Choose pictures that show your client dogs in action on their walks, having a great time. On each month include a walking-related tip about how to make walks more fun and safe, remove ticks, protect dogs' feet in the snow, etc. You can include the dates of the local dog festival or parade, national dog day, etc. And reinforce your referral sources and court new ones by highlighting a dog-friendly business each month as well.

Use branded trading cards

This is a great way to get clients to tell friends, family, and colleagues about you. Create branded trading cards for each of your client dogs, modeled after baseball cards. Put the dog's picture on one side, with their stats on the other: name, breed, age, favorite walking activity, favorite walking place, best dog friend, etc. Include a bit of humor by listing the dog's nickname or a little known fact about him, such as a love of eating grass or fear of squirrels.

Be sure the card is branded with your logo and colors and includes your website address. Give clients plenty of cards to share with others to show off their dog.

You can create these in batches, creating one to three each quarter. Leave small stacks around your service area in dog businesses, cafés, etc. for curious dog lovers and kids to pick up. Such cards will be many times more memorable than a plain old business card!

Wear logo clothing

You are your own best advertisement as you walk down the street or trail with your well-behaved charges. Don't miss this opportunity. Have your logo silkscreened or embroidered on to t-shirts or polos, sweatshirts, and a winter jacket or rain coat. People are more likely to stop you for a business card if it's clear you're a professional. (And wait until you hand them one of your trading cards instead!)

Arrange dog park cleanups

This marketing idea is about as inexpensive as they come. Don your logo clothing, grab your poop bags, and do some community service by cleaning up a local park or trail. Bring your business cards (or, much better, your "How to Choose a Professional Dog Walker" flier or branded trading cards) to share with people you meet as you work.

You can push this idea further by inviting other dog pros and businesses to join you, creating a networking opportunity. And let the local paper and bloggers know what you're up to. If they don't show, take pictures (don't forget the before and after angle!) to send to the local paper along with captions and a short write-up.

Social media

How does it work?

It's easy to get swept up in the social media craze and buy into the notion that it's a panacea for marketing success, that if you just launch a Facebook page, business will come marching your way. Unfortunately it's not quite that simple. Even top social media marketing gurus agree social media is no replacement for on-the-ground marketing. Social media is something you add to your marketing plan, not something you replace it with.

This makes sense when you understand how social media works, particularly in our industry. Most people aren't trawling the Internet looking for dog walkers to follow or friend. If someone becomes your Facebook fan or Twitter follower, it's most likely he or she already knows you. That person is a client, or possibly a serious potential client looking to learn a bit more about you. In short, social media in our industry is largely about retention marketing. It plays to the folks already on your side by maintaining contact and reinforcing their loyalty to your brand.

As such, it can't be actively relied on to bring new business your way. Like word of mouth, it takes a while to build a social media presence to the point where you begin generating new business, particularly when you consider what a small-volume business dog walking is. (You will take on a relatively small number of clients over the life of your business compared to the volume of people a retail shop might see, for example.) But staying in touch with current and past clients is valuable in itself to keep clients loyal to your services, let them know about new services you may choose to offer, and keep you in their minds. They are more likely to refer others to you if their relationship with you is strong and active—and that's where the new business will eventually come from.

Which social media tools to use

With this in mind, let's consider a few of the best social media options. New social media tools are launched all the time, but social media is a time-consuming endeavor to do properly, so pick and choose your outlets carefully. Here are some of the best bets for dog walkers.

Facebook is the current king of social media sites, a network of one billion users (at the time of writing) who create online profiles, link to friends old and new, share news, photos, and videos. Create a fan page for your business, and use it to share updates or information that others might find helpful or entertaining. Keep in mind the "social" in social media; unlike more traditional marketing methods, the businesses most successful at social media eschew self-promotion and instead concentrate on building relationships. The focus shifts to the consumer, and solving her problems. Provide the occasional free article on humane anti-pull devices, point out a fellow dog walker's site when your client list is full, or answer a question about your holiday policies.

A **blog** is a website featuring regular posts, or updates, and is an excellent tool for growing your brand. Many domain hosts make blogging easy, featuring easy integration with blogging platforms like Wordpress, Tumblr, or Blogger—platforms that take care of the programming for you; just write a quick post, then hit Publish. In fact, more and more businesses set up their websites on one of these content management system (CMS) platforms. Wordpress, for example, includes a sophisticated set of plug-ins, or tools, that can improve your SEO, tag your posts with relevant keywords, and keep track of your number of visitors. Frequently updated blogs attract the most visitors, so consider budgeting a couple of hours a week to blogging. Include links to helpful articles by respected peers in your industry, photos from your walks, or funny stories of dogs you've been walking. Let your writing reflect your own speaking style; a casual, personable writing voice is more likely attract loyal readers and potential clients.

Twitter is the social network for short attention spans, a running stream of tweets (posts) of 140 characters or less. Other users can choose to follow your tweets, which will show up on their stream. Social media is better at strengthening existing relationships than attracting new ones, and Twitter makes it easy to open dialogues, both public and private, with clients and other dog pros. Again, limit self-promotion to about 15% of your overall posts, or you run the risk of getting tuned out. Answer a frequently asked question, tell a joke, post a quick free walking tip, or share info about a favorite trail or walking route. Follow and comment on the tweets of peers in the dog professions, check up on current and former clients, and you'll strengthen those connections most likely to give you the best word of mouth.

LinkedIn focuses on professional networking. Users create profiles that resemble employment resumes, and link to friends, co-workers, and employers, both current and past. Link to your trainer peers, the owner of your favorite daycare facility, or fellow students from your dog walking academy. If you prefer to work with small dogs, establish ties with that trainer who specializes in them, and send each other clients.

YouTube is a massive online library for videos and can be a terrific resource for introducing your business to potential clients. Videos are also a powerful search engine optimization tool to help people find you first. YouTube videos run the full spectrum of production values, and with the popularity of video editing software, you can throw together your own short video on your computer in a few hours. Share a typical day in the life of a dog walker, or a profile of one of your walking dogs and her people to show the positive effect your walking service has had on both. Never underestimate the appeal of cute dogs; videos that go viral (i.e., become insanely popular, widely linked to, and distributed by fans online) often feature animals. Create a profile with a link to your business site and embed your videos on your blog or Facebook fan page.

Flickr is an online photo and video management and sharing application. You can upload photos to the site via numerous methods and share them with clients or the public. Other users can comment on your photos or subscribe to your photo stream. Tag your photos with relevant keywords and embed your photos or videos on your business site.

Pinterest is a visual content-sharing service that allows you to share your interests, inspiration, and expertise by "pinning" (i.e., posting) images, videos, and articles to so-called pinboards. Think of it as social storyboarding or a show-and-tell bonanza. Each board is a themed collection of images about anything that interests or inspires you: dog products you love (you can go to town and have a board for each product: beds, food, collars and leashes, treats, etc.), dog statistics, holiday-themed boards (Santa Paws, Easter Dogs, Howl-O-Ween Dogs), famous dogs, covers of great dog books, a meet-the-team board with photos of you and any staff members, photos from dog park cleanups or other events, or photos from your favorite rescue group or local shelter. When the subject matter (dogs!) is so utterly interesting and photogenic, the possibilities are endless. You can post your own photos and, as most people do, also find interesting images and informative content on other sites or Pinterest streams. This is a fun and wildly popular service where dog lovers number in the millions.

Instagram is another image-based social media platform on the rise. What began as a fun way to pass pictures, videos, and short messages to friends and family is fast becoming the new thing in social media marketing. Instagram is particularly suited to dog walkers, allowing you to easily share the day's walking adventures with clients and followers as they happen, via the Instagram network and other social networks including Facebook, Twitter and Flickr. Set up an Instagram profile for your business, then share pictures of dogs having a great time and videos of them frolicking, along with caption-length messages: "It's such a gorgeous day we decided to visit the pond for a swim. This is Duke getting his paws wet." Or "It's Spot's first day out with the group—here he is making friends with Fido."

Using social media

Like any type of marketing, social media should be tackled with a strategy. Think about your content before you begin. Have 25 to 50 blog topics brainstormed before you start a blog. Create a list of content categories for Facebook before you launch your page, and a list of places to look for that content. Set aside time in your schedule each week to hunt for and create content to ensure your social media presence will be active and consistent. Your goal is to build and maintain brand loyalty, and it's easy to undermine it instead with inconsistency. A blog or Twitter feed that hasn't been updated in weeks looks unprofessional and implies a poorly run business.

Remember that social media is about engagement, entertainment, and a bit of education. As with your newsletter, keep the content about your services to a minimum—no more than 15%—or you risk sounding like a commercial and losing fans and followers. Think about how you can show what you do while entertaining and being useful to your audience. Talk about walking and give walking-related equipment tips and information, share which dog-related and dog-friendly businesses and products you recommend, flag upcoming dog events and national dog-themed days, pass on information about dogs or dog issues from the local, national, or even international news, and search out the best dog jokes, cutest dog photos, and funniest dog stories on the Internet.

Be social

Part of your job is to engage with your audience, to get them talking, asking questions, commenting on your posts and each other's. Check your social media tools daily to stay actively engaged in the conversation yourself. Answer questions promptly and thank people for positive comments. Go a step further with tricks like posting questions and polls for your followers: Where are their favorite walking spots? Which trail should you take the dogs on tomorrow? Guess the breed(s) of this dog?

For the 15% of your content specific to your business, keep the direct service entreaties (asking for referrals or letting people know about your new weekend hikes, for example) rare. Find ways to show-don't-tell about your services. For example, share fun stories from the life of a dog walker, post pictures and videos and profiles of the dogs in your care that your clients might be inclined to pass on to their friends and family and co-workers for a little bragging time.

Other online marketing

Distribute an e-newsletter
E-newsletters are as important to retention marketing as the print version is to public marketing, but the format is a bit different. Rather than the two- or four-page quarterly print version, your email newsletter should be monthly and short. Share a quick tip, or an excerpt from an interesting article about dogs, or a humorous or thoughtful anecdote from one of your walks. Put together a fun profile of one of your walking dogs, complete with a picture. Include a short call for referrals to friends and family. That's it. Keeping it short and entertaining means clients are more likely to read the next one—and hopefully to pass it along, too.

Add yourself to referral sites
These national (and sometimes local) websites with built-in referral databases position themselves as the go-to place for people trying to find the best this, that, or the other. Some are large, general, and exclusive directory sites you have to apply to, that cover all manner of services. Others are referral sites focused on a particular kind of service, such as dog walking or pet sitting. Not everyone looking for something on the internet will do a specific, logical search that includes their geographic location. When potential clients simply tell Google to look for "dog walking" there's a good chance they'll end up on one of these referral sites, where they can then search for a walker in their local area. If they do, they'll find you—if you're listed. It's sort of like 1-800-DENTIST for the 21st century.

Getting listed on most of these sites is free; a few come with low annual fees that are generally worthwhile. What's a $50 marketing expense if it gains you even one ongoing dog walking client? And having large sites with lots of traffic linked to yours can also boost your website's search rankings, helping you to appear higher on the page when people do remember to search by location. See the Resources section at the back of the book for a list of referral sites that include or specialize in dog walker listings.

Getting ready

You have your message and you know who it's for. You've decided which marketing vehicles will help you deliver that message. But before you put yourself out there, you have to make sure you look good. If you intend to have a professional dog walking business, it has to look the part. That means a visual brand and a website—both done professionally.

Your logo

Your logo—the visual representation of your business name—is the centerpiece of your visual brand. It, and the design work done around it on your website and marketing materials, will become your calling card, so to speak. The best logos are kept simple and easily recognizable. Your visual branding should be consistent across all your materials, using the same layouts, colors, and fonts so people begin to recognize your brand as they come across it.

Your website

Your website has two jobs to do for you: to help people find you and to help close the sale. The former is all about search engine optimization, or SEO. When a potential client goes searching for a dog walker online, you want your site to come up high in the list Google or any other search engine returns to her—not buried on the bottom of the seventh page. SEO is a complicated and ever-changing field. There are some simple things you can do—like making sure the most obvious keywords (dog walking, dog walker, and the towns you serve) are present in your website copy. But if you work in a competitive market, it may be worthwhile to hire an SEO expert to set your site up for success.

Getting people to your site—through SEO and through your community marketing—is only half the battle. Once potential clients have found it, your site has to convince them they're in the right place and to call or email you to get started. Your website is your most important marketing and sales tool. Fail to give it the attention it deserves, and you undermine all your other marketing efforts.

Your site needs to be easy to read and navigate. It should make a strong, effective case for dog walking and for you, and make it easy for people to contact you once it has.

Don't do it yourself

Given the importance of these tools, this is no time for DIY. You're asking professional people to entrust you with a treasured family member. A clip-art logo and homemade website won't do the trick. If you want to make money as a professional dog walker it makes sense—and is worth every penny—to invest a bit in your business start up. A strong visual brand and an effective website built by professionals who specialize in this work are key. Unless you're a professional graphic designer, hire someone to create your logo. Unless you're a professional website designer, hire someone to design your site. Unless you're a professional website programmer or SEO expert, hire people who are. And unless you're a strong writer with a marketing background and an understanding of how website copy works, hire a professional writer to produce the copy for your site. I can't stress enough what a mistake it is to try to save money on these steps. You can find contact information for logo designers, website designers and developers, website writers, and search engine optimization specialists in the Resources section. These companies specialize in working with small dog businesses. They understand the industry and price themselves appropriately for working within it.

Work ON your business

One of the biggest mistakes I see dog business owners make is working too much in the business, not nearly enough *on* it. This is understandable; dog lovers become business owners to spend their days working with dogs, not to be marketing managers. But if you want to play with dogs for a living, you have to have clients willing to entrust their dogs to you. And that means marketing.

The good news is that I've seen many dog pros start businesses with a dread of marketing and then, over time, become marketing junkies. As I mentioned in Chapter 2, reinforced behavior increases—this is true for us humans, too. As you learn to market your business and are rewarded for it with new clients, you'll probably find yourself wanting to do more marketing.

In the meantime, plan to set aside a regular block of time (or a couple) each week to focus on marketing. Plan to spend at least four hours a week, every week, on marketing. And if you have more time, use it. The more marketing you do, the faster your business will grow.

Chapter 13

The Professional Dog Walker

What makes a dog walker a professional? Is it a passion for dogs? Charging clients for dog walking services? Having the right vehicle and policies? Creating an effective marketing plan? Though all these things are important, none push a walker into the professional realm. Professional dog walkers recognize that loving dogs and walking them for money isn't enough. They know the industry lacks regulation and set standards, and they choose to go beyond what is expected or required to offer the best for their human and canine clients while contributing to the growth of a budding profession.

Professional dog walkers share these characteristics:

A commitment to education and professional development

True professionals in any industry recognize the hubris in assuming there isn't more to learn. They seek out educational opportunities throughout their careers, regardless of how much experience or peer recognition they amass. This approach makes particular sense in the dog industry; we're working with a separate species, after all. If you've made it all the way to the end of this book, I'm guessing you agree. You'll find numerous classes, books, and DVDs in the Resources section to continue your professional education.

A commitment to ethical and safe dog care practices

Keep groups small. It's tempting financially to take as many dogs as you can fit in a vehicle or as many leashes as you can hold, but that will inevitably backfire in the form of increased incidents, which mean vet bills, unhappy clients, complaints to the city or park district, and a poor reputation.

Avoid interaction with others. Keep your dogs focused on you and, if you're walking groups, each other. They're out with you to get exercise, not to make new friends and greet strangers. The only way to be absolutely sure a dog doesn't bite someone is to avoid interaction. And while the dogs you walk may be tremendously friendly, you can't predict or control the behavior or other dogs and people. "Better safe than sorry" is the mantra here.

Screen and group carefully. You and the dogs will have a better, safer time if you group dogs appropriately according to size (remember the 50% rule!) and temperament.

Be positive. Use only scientifically sound, humane, positive training approaches and equipment. Remember, you're walking someone else's "baby."

A commitment to ethical business practices

Set clear policies. Make sure your clients understand your policies—what they are and why you have them. Then enforce them; there's no point having policies if you don't use them.

Go above and beyond. Always over-deliver on customer service. Communicate daily to let clients know about their dog's walk. Share helpful seasonal pointers. Bake dog biscuits for the holidays. Put out a client e-newsletter with helpful tips for weekend walks. In short, be present in your clients' lives.

Respect your colleagues. Never speak poorly of fellow dog pros; it only makes you look unprofessional. Consider and treat fellow dog pros as colleagues rather than competitors. Dog walking isn't a volume-based business; there are plenty of dogs to go around. And if you work for others, remember that those clients belong to your employer. When it's time to go out on your own, don't start your new business by hurting someone else's.

Be an ambassador. Every moment you're out walking, you represent not only your own business, but dog walkers and the dog walking industry in general. Keep your dogs engaged and focused on you, move off the trail to let others pass, and avoid interactions whenever possible—there can't be an incident if no one is within reach. Ideally every person who comes into contact with you and your dogs, every person sharing the sidewalk, trail, park, or beach, should go home feeling all the better about dogs and dog walkers for it.

A final word

You've chosen a great way to make a living. Your colleagues are four-leggeds who are delighted to see you every day. Your office is the great outdoors. You have very little paperwork and no major deadlines. There are challenges, yes. Dogs do unpredictable things. You probably spend more time driving than you'd like. And there are days spent walking in the rain. But as one of our Dog Walking Academy grads once said, "The worst day dog walking is better than the best day in an office." Very true. So congratulations—to you, to your human clients, and to the dogs who eagerly await your arrival each day.

Resources for the
Professional Dog Walker

1. Business Resources

Insurance Agents
Dennis Stowers
dstowers@mourer-foster.com
800 686 2663 ext. 230

Legal Assistance
Heidi Meinzer
heidi@meinzerlaw.com
www.meinzerlaw.com
Trademarks: Legal Care for Your Business and Product Name, www.nolopress.com
The Employer's Legal Handbook, www.nolopress.com

Contracts
Business CD for Walkers & Sitters www.dogtec.org

Bookkeepers & Accountants
Dollars & Scents www.dog-pro-cpa.com
A full service bookkeeping and tax preparation service exclusively for dog professionals

Bookkeeping Help   www.bookkeepinghelp.com
US and Canadian directory for bookkeepers, accountants, and tax preparers

Marketing Designers
dog*tec maintains an active, up-to-date list of writers, logo designers, and website developers who specialize in working with dog businesses. Email info@dogtec.org or call 510.525.2547 for free referrals.

Online Marketing Opportunities
Dogasaur www.dogasaur.com

Dogwalker.com www.dogwalker.com

Embarkly www.embarkly.com

Find Pet Care www.findpetcare.com

Rover.com www.rover.com

Red Dog Classifieds www.reddogclassifieds.com

Branded Poop Bags
Bio Buddy www.bio-buddy.com

Branded Trading Cards
Custom Trading Cards www.custom-tradingcards.com

Distribute poop bags
This is a great project for creating good will and brand recognition. Have your logo and website address printed on (preferably biodegradable) poop bags, then hang plastic dispensers (like the kind you might use in your kitchen to store used grocery bags) throughout your target neighborhoods and local parks. You provide a useful service while getting some good marketing done.

Software and Apps
BettaWalka software www.bettawalka.com

Bluewave Professional Pet Sitter software www.professionalpetsitter.com

ICE for Pets app www.iceforpets.com

Paw Loyalty software www.pawloyalty.com

PetPro software www.petprosoftware.net

Pet Sit Click software www.petsitclick.com

PetTech PetSaver app www.pettech.net

Power Pet Sitter software www.powersitter.com

Veriwalk app www.veriwalk.com

Mental Stimulation Toys

Canine Genius dog toys www.caninegenius.com

Doggie Prodigy www.doggieprodigy.com

Kongs www.kongcompany.com

Nina Ottosson puzzle toys www.nina-ottosson.com

Premier dog toys (Tug-A-Jug, Busy Buddy, etc.) www.premier.com

Smarter Toys (Buster Cube, Atomic Treat Ball, IQ Treat Ball) www.ourpets.com

dog*tec Business Support Services

www.dogtec.org
info@dogtec.org
veronica@dogtec.org
Business consulting
Business support products, including the Business CD for Walkers & Sitters
Newsletter Service
Monthly Minute free email business newsletter—email info@dogtec.org for a free subscription or sign up at www.dogtec.org
Free article archive of business advice for dog pros at www.dogtec.org

2. Education Resources

Schools & Certification

dog*tec Dog Walking Academy   www.dogtec.org

Continuing Education Seminars & Web Seminars

Association of Pet Dog Trainers   www.apdt.com

Association of Pet Sitting Excellence www.petsittingexcellence.com

Dogs of Course   www.dogsofcourse.com

Dog Seminars Directory www.dogseminarsdirectory.com

dog*tec   www.dogtec.org

Recommended Reading

Books
Culture Clash, Jean Donaldson

Canine Behavior, Barbara Handelman

Canine Body Language: A Photographic Guide, Brenda Aloff

Dog Language: An Encyclopedia of Canine Behavior, 2nd Edition, Roger Abrantes

How to Run a Dog Business: Putting Your Career Where Your Heart Is, Veronica Boutelle

Minding Your Dog Business: A Practical Guide to Business Success for Dog Professionals, Veronica Boutelle & Rikke Jorgensen

Off Leash Dog Play—A Complete Guide to Safety and Fun, Robin K. Bennett & Susan Briggs

The Other End of the Leash, Patricia McConnell

The Power of Positive Dog Training, Pat Miller

Reaching the Animal Mind, Karen Pryor

Reactive Rover, Kim Moeller

Articles
American Veterinary Society of Animal Behavior statement on puppy socialization www.avsabonline.org

"Alpha-Schmalpha" by Pat Miller, *Whole Dog Journal*, December 2011 www.whole-dog-journal.com

CDs & DVDs
Reactive Rover, Kim Moeller

What is My Dog Saying?, Carol A. Byrnes

Websites
Operation Socialization www.operationsocialization.com

Book and DVD Sources
Dogwise   www.dogwise.com

Tawzer Video   www.tawzervideo.com

Associations
Association of Pet Sitting Excellence (APSE) www.petsittingexcellence.com

National Association of Professional Pet Sitters (NAPPS)   www.napps.org

Pet Sitters International (PSI)   www.psi.org

3. Budget Considerations

A word on business plans and budgets.
Unless you are seeking funding, you will not need a formal business plan. Following the advice in each chapter of this book will reward you with an informal business plan to guide you as you move forward to start or grow your enterprise. Should you require a formal plan, you'll soon realize that there are more templates to choose from than you could possibly need. It's best to ask the funding sources you will be petitioning what they want to see in a solid plan. If they have a specific template, all the better. In the absence of such direction, Palo Alto Software has a good product with several dog-related samples. www.paloaltosoftware.com

Here I have provided a basic list of potential start-up and ongoing costs you should be aware of when doing your feasibility math.

Start-Up Costs

Vehicle (if needed)

Communication
- cell phone purchase
- initial internet fees—service installation

Initial Marketing
- website development
- URL purchase
- design and printing
- advertising, if doing
- other one time intial project costs specific to your plans

Professional Fees & Assistance

- paperwork fees
- contracts
- accountancy support
- lawyer, if using

Education

- school and seminar fees
- books and DVDs
- business coaching support

Office Supplies

- hardware—computer, printer, etc.
- software—Quickbooks Pro, client management software

Dog Supplies

- leashes, tags, first aid kit, mental stimulation toys if needed, etc.

Ongoing Costs

Vehicle

- maintenance
- gas

Communication

- cell phone service
- internet service

Marketing

- website maintenance, hosting fees, URL renewal
- ongoing project costs
- replacement printing
- advertising, if doing

Professional Fees & Assistance

- professional insurance
- accountancy and/or bookkeeping

Professional Development & Continuing Education

- association fees
- seminars
- books & DVDs
- business support services

Office Supplies

Dog Supplies

- treats, replacement leashes, etc.

Employment Costs, if using employees

- pay
- payroll taxes and fees

4. Annotated Start-Up To Do List

Legalities & Liabilities

	To Do	Notes	Source

1.	Check Name Availability	Be sure the name you want to use is free for use. Do a search on the national trademark sight, your state trademark and LLC/corporation site, your county site, and check to see what domain names are available (.com, etc.).	www.uspto.gov
			
			your secretary of state site
			
			your county clerk site
			
			Domain name search and registration:
			
			    www.register.com
			
			    www.1and1.com
			
			    www.dreamhost.com
			
			    www.namecheap.com

	To Do	Notes	Source
2.	File For LLC Status (optional)	This is an optional step you may choose to take to increase your liability protection. You can convert to an LLC at any time. If you file as an LLC be sure to use the full business name as the "applicant" on all other steps below.	Download forms from your secretary of state site For help: www.dogtec.org www.NoloPress.com local lawyer
3.	Business License	Remember to proactively file a home-based business exemption if needed	Download forms from your city website or call or walk in for them
4.	Fictitious Business Name	Read instructions carefully—multiple copies are often required. You will probably need to run an announcement in a local paper. If neither the FBN nor the business license needs the other one completed first, go ahead and file both at the same time	Download forms from your county clerk website or call or walk in for them
5.	Get Your EIN	If you've filed as an LLC or if you plan to have employees, you need an EIN. Otherwise it is not required. If you apply online the form number is SS-4.	Apply online at www.irs.gov Or get your EIN over the phone by calling 800 829 4933

	To Do	Notes	Source
6.	Open Business Bank Account	This is highly recommended for all businesses and required for LLCs Call your bank ahead to schedule an appointment. Be sure to ask them what paperwork to bring along.	Local bank of your choice
7.	Join a Professional Association	This is great for continuing education opportunities and it helps to professionalize your business as well as push the industry forward.	Membership also provides access to professional insurance. www.petsittingexcellence.com www.napps.com www.psi.com
8.	Obtain Insurance	If you're going to start walking dogs before you can get the first 7 steps completed, get insurance first. You can always change the name on your policy if you need to.	Dennis Stowers dstowers@mourer-foster.com
9.	Purchase Contracts	Have contracts in hand before you take on a client. If you will be interviewing clients before this step, move this step up!	www.dogtec.org
10.	Service Mark Your Business Name (optional)	Dog walkers can service mark at the state level. Doing so is optional.	Download forms from your secretary of state site

	To Do	Notes	Source
11.	Learn LLC Rules & Requirements	Learn what you need to know to keep your LLC protection intact.	www.dogtec.org www.NoloPress.com

Marketing

While waiting for various paperwork to come back from the offices you've sent it out to, you can get to work on your marketing. See the Marketing chapter for more detailed instructions.

	To Do	Notes	Source
1.	Define Your Services	Decide exactly what you're going to offer, down to the details. Consider a specialized niche. Be clear about who your target clients are.	www.dogtec.org
2.	Develop Your Marketing Message	How will you describe what you do to those who will use your services? What makes you different? What benefits do clients stand to gain?	
3.	Develop Your Marketing Projects	These are the vehicles that will get your message out to your audience. Choose several projects and pick one or two to implement first.	
4.	Develop Marketing Materials	Now that you know what your projects are, you know what materials you need. Engage a designer for a professionally branded look.	See list of designers on page 134.

Rates, Policies, & Systems

	To Do	Notes	Source
1.	Research Local Rates	Call other local service providers (or ask a friend to call for you) to find out what they charge. Be sure to get details about their services—type and length of walks, etc.	
2.	Set Your Rates	Keep all variables in mind: local rates, how your services are different or unique, what you need and want to be paid. You do not have to "apologize" for being new through your rates!	www.dogtec.org
3.	Write Your Policies	Put together policies for payment, cancellation, geographical boundaries, etc. Write your policies for the future! You may not be busy now, but you will be. Make sure your policies will fit the needs of a growing business.	

	To Do	Notes	Source
4.	Design Systems and Develop or Purchase Materials for Them	You need systems and materials for phone screening, your initial intake or interview process, payment and general bookkeeping, ongoing record keeping, dog groupings and routes if applicable, client homework if applicable, etc.	www.dogtec.org www.dog-pro-cpa.com Quickbooks Pro software www.pawloyalty.com www.petsitclick.com www.veriwalk.com

Scheduling

	To Do	Notes	Source
1.	List All Business Duties	This includes client and dog care time as well as marketing and admin work.	
2,	List Everything Else	Include any other responsibilities, including any part- or full-time work, family duties, and recreational activities you wish to prioritize.	
3.	Devise a Schedule	Work to accommodate your business and personal needs as efficiently as possible.	
4.	Try It Out	Give the schedule a go and make adjustments as needed.	

About the Author

Veronica Boutelle, MA, CTC, is creator and co-president of dog*tec, the industry's leading business support company. In addition to teaching the Dog Walking Academy, Veronica gives business seminars for dog pros across the country and consults with dog pros one-on-one to help start and grow their businesses. Veronica is the author of *How to Run a Dog Business: Putting Your Career Where Your Heart Is*, co-author of *Minding Your Dog Business: A Practical Guide to Business Success for Dog Professionals*, and writes "The Business End of the Leash" column for *The APDT Chronicle of the Dog*. She is the former Director of Behavior and Training for the San Francisco SPCA. Veronica lives on the Oregon coast with her husband and "the cutest little old lady dog in the world," their Whippet mix, Zeppa (aka Stripey or The Bean). She grows dahlias in her spare time.

INDEX

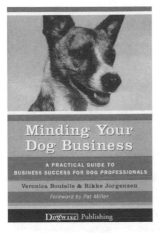

Minding Your Dog Business

A Practical Guide to Business Success for Dog Professionals
Veronica Boutelle and Rikke Jorgensen

Setting up and running a successful dog-related business is an achievement in itself, but building a business with staying power that can succeed over the long run is the ultimate test for a dog pro. dogTEC's Veronica Boutelle and Rikke Jorgenson new book will help guide you as you work to build your dog business, whether you are a trainer, a dog walker, a dog sitter, or a daycare owner. Of special interest to many of you dog pros will be the up to date information on the latest in marketing technologies and techniques as well as how to manage your business during economic downturns. A truly great resource for dog pros.

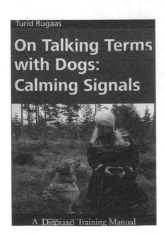

On Talking Terms with Dogs

Calming Signals, 2nd Ed.
Turid Rugaas

Norwegian dog trainer and behaviorist Turid Rugaas is a noted expert on canine body language, notably "calming signals," which are signals dogs use to avoid conflict, invite play, and communicate a wide range of information to other dogs and people. These are the dogs' attempt to defuse situations that otherwise might result in fights or aggression.

Companion DVD, 'Calming Signals: What Your Dog Tells You,' DTB788, is also available. The DVD shows footage of many calming signals, how dogs use them, and how you can use them to calm your dog.

Dogwise.com your source for quality books, ebooks, DVDs, training tools and treats.

We've been selling to the dog fancier for more than 25 years and we carefully screen our products for quality information, safety, durability and FUN! You'll find something for every level of dog enthusiast on our website www.dogwise.com or drop by our store in Wenatchee, Washington.

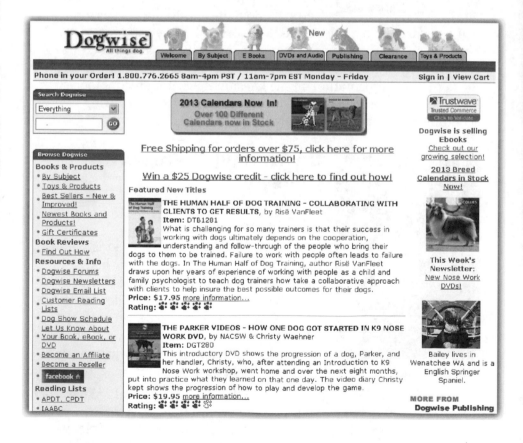